UNDERSTANDING CHINESE SOCIETY

Changes and Transformations

Series on Contemporary China (ISSN: 1793-0847)

Series Editors: Joseph Fewsmith *(Boston University)*
Zheng Yongnian *(East Asian Institute, National University of Singapore)*

*To view the complete list of the published volumes in the series, please visit:
http://www.worldscientific.com/series/scc

Series on Contemporary China – Vol. 37

UNDERSTANDING CHINESE SOCIETY
Changes and Transformations

Eileen Yuk-ha Tsang

City University of Hong Kong, Hong Kong

World Scientific

JERSEY · LONDON · SINGAPORE · BEIJING · SHANGHAI · HONG KONG · TAIPEI · CHENNAI · TOKYO

Published by

World Scientific Publishing Co. Pte. Ltd.

5 Toh Tuck Link, Singapore 596224

USA office: 27 Warren Street, Suite 401-402, Hackensack, NJ 07601

UK office: 57 Shelton Street, Covent Garden, London WC2H 9HE

Library of Congress Cataloging-in-Publication Data
Tsang, Eileen Yuk-Ha.
   Understanding Chinese society : changes and transformations / Eileen Yuk-ha Tsang
(City University of Hong Kong, Hong Kong).
      pages cm. -- (Series on contemporary China ; vol. 37)
   ISBN 978-9814644853 (alk. paper)
   1. China--Social conditions--2000-   2. Social change--China. I. Title.
   HN733.5.T736 2015
   306.0951--dc23

                                               2015017665

British Library Cataloguing-in-Publication Data
A catalogue record for this book is available from the British Library.

In-house Editors: Dr. Sree Meenakshi Sajani/Qi Xiao

Typeset by Stallion Press
Email: enquiries@stallionpress.com

Printed in Singapore

For My Parents and My Soulmate

Contents

About the Author

Eileen Yuk-Ha Tsang

Eileen Yuk-Ha Tsang, PhD, is an Assistant Professor in the Department of Applied Social Sciences, City University of Hong Kong, Hong Kong. She earned her PhD in Sociology from the University of Birmingham, UK. Her research interests include Chinese Studies, Sex and Gender, Social Stratification and Mobility, Globalization and Cultural Sociology. Her research interests are related to Cultural and political Sociology of China's emerging middle class, Sociology of sex and gender, Sociology of consumption and popular culture. Her recent major publications about the new Chinese middle class include "The Chinese New Middle Class and Green NGOs in South China: Vanguards of *Guanxi* (Connections)-Seeking, Laggards in Promoting Social Causes?" [*China: An International Journal* 11, No. 2 (August 2013): 155–169 (with Pak K. Lee)]; "The Quest for Higher Education by the Chinese Middle Class: Retrenching Social Mobility?" [*Higher Education* 66, No. 6 (December 2013): 653–168]; and *The New Middle Class in China: Consumption, Politics and the Market Economy* (Palgrave Macmillan, 2014).

Foreword

Eileen Tsang has taken on a huge task to make China — and its people — understandable to non-Chinese. No small feat. I have lived in Hong Kong and China for over a decade and have also witnessed the awakening and rise of this superpower.

I had the pleasure of meeting and working with Eileen during my time as the Dean of the Division of Humanities and Social Sciences at the United International College in Zhuhai, China. I found that she has unique strengths as a writer and a storyteller. Through her careful observations and naturally curious nature, she has insights that are here conveyed through words and pictures. The reader will find this book fuses the distinct writing styles, that of the professional storyteller and the academic scholar as a sociologist. Together, this book weaves a tapestry of ideas and experiences that capture the changes and trends in today's China.

Eileen Tsang is an accomplished sociologist who provides the academic anchor for the text. She did her ethnographic interviews and in-depth interviews and places them within the larger cultural context of how these changes are transforming Chinese society. Throughout this book she also summarizes much of her research findings, and together, she gives the reader a clear picture of what is happening in the People's Republic of China. She also makes vivid descriptions on the transformations of the Chinese society from pre-reform China to post-reform China.

Eileen has combined her talents to create a significant work of knowledge. It is both enjoyable to read. I hope the readers enjoy reading it as much as I did, and through it, better appreciate today's China!

Professor Jeff Wilkinson
Chair and Professor, Department of Communication
University of Toledo, Ohio (USA)

Introduction

China has experienced robust changes since 2000. Before 1978, China was weak — economically, politically, and diplomatically. China was extremely isolated before 1978, and had only a few diplomatic allies such as North Korea, Russia, and Vietnam. But since the year 2000, significant changes have taken place.

Recently, many books about China have focused mainly on the history, culture, and politics of this great country. Therefore, for many professors and students it is difficult to find textbooks which explore and analyze the changing Chinese society. This book's focus is to meet that need; it will examine in-depth the various socio-economic and socio-cultural issues of China from the scholarly perspectives of Sociology, Cultural Studies, as well as China Studies.

China is the interest of many Europeans, Americans, and other foreigners. However, many of these individuals overlook the complex socio-economic and socio-cultural elements of the country. I am a Hong-Kong Chinese and my research specialties include China Studies, the new Chinese middle class, and popular culture within Chinese societies. From 2008 to 2011, I conducted interviews in this book. This book provides first-hand information to readers to understand Chinese Society in more vivid, dynamic, and practical ways. It examines many different facets of the Chinese society ranging from famous landmarks, popular customs, festivals, food, and daily chores, to the author's impressions of the striking cultural differences between the regions.

I acknowledge and I am grateful to Mc Graw Hill for releasing the copyright for part of the chapters from the book *Blending East and West, The Changing Chinese Society* (Singapore: Mc Graw-Hill, 2012). I also acknowledge Palgrave Macmillan for releasing the copyright for Chapter 1, Chapter 2, and Chapter 5.

This book introduces the societal characteristics of Chinese society, both past and present, through the analysis of the political, social, and economic changes that have affected China since 1949. It includes examination of various changes in family and kinship, women and education, middle class formation, and the emergence of the Chinese new middle class (See Photo 1). This module also

Photo 1:   The blending West and East are everywhere in China. The sky-scrapers and Chinese lanterns are one of the examples of the blending East and West. This becomes an interesting culture in downtown Guangdong.

focuses on newly emerging socio-cultural changes such as consumerism, beauty myths, cultural/medical tourism, popular culture, and the mass media. This book will also be useful to readers who want to know more about the business culture in mainland China.

Part I is the Basic Institutions of the Chinese societies, in Chapters 3 to 6. Chapter 1 focuses on Chinese society in pre-reform China. We introduce different peculiar features in Mao's China. These features include *hukou*, *danwei*, and People's Communes in Mao's China. Chapter 2 examines Chinese society in post-reform China and institutional reform. This deals with the features in post-Mao China since 1978.

Part II of this book, in Chapters 4 to 6, covers the Socio-Economic Changes in the Chinese Societies. Chapter 3 is titled Chinese Family and Kinship: Yesterday and Today. Chapter 4 concerns Chinese Women and Education. Chapter 5 covers the Emergence of the Chinese New Middle Class. Chapter 6 is about Governmentality and Conspicuous Consumption.

Part III — including Chapters 7 to 12 — focuses on Social-Cultural Changes in Chinese Societies. Chapter 7 is about Institutionalization of *Guanxi* (connections). Chapter 8 is about Consumerism, the Pursuit of Beauty, and Medical Tourism in Today's China. Chapter 9 shares the Legacy of "Leftover Lady". Chapter 10 is about the Masculinity Crisis of the Young Generation in post-Reform China. It describes the leftover men issues and masculinity crisis of the ant tribes in post-Reform China. Chapter 11 related to the Corruption and NGOs in China. Last but not least, Chapter 12 contains Information about Popular Culture, Media, and Society in post-Reform China.

This book consists of diverse types of information about the changes and transformation of the changing Chinese societies since 1978. It can be useful for scholars and students working in the fields of Area Studies and Chinese Studies, and Chinese public policy. It is also recommended as an essential supplementary source for the studies of consumer marketing, consumer psychology, and courses directly related to Globalization, Popular Culture, and Liberal Arts.

The most important mission of this book is to address the special interests of the Western audience who wish to learn more about China, Macau, and Hong Kong but have not had a chance to go to these places. It will hopefully become the "must read" book for Western or European audiences, politicians, and businesspeople. The book can also be used as an overview of China for a general audience.

Finally, this book is especially dedicated to you, the reader, as a member of our Chinese Studies community. We hope that you find a blend of inspiration and insights that will help define your interests in China Studies if you work, live, or study in mainland China.

Part I
Basic Institutions
of the Chinese Societies

Chapter 1

The Chinese Society
in Pre-Reform China

The Chinese society that I knew growing up is completely different than the China today (see Figure 1). During my generation in the 1980s, China was removed from the world stage and the West. Consequently, little was known about the country. Sometimes, the mass media of the US created creative, but inaccurate images of China. It is easy to recall a comic book character, "The Yellow Claw" who represented an image that a number of foreigners, especially Americans, may have believed (Littlefield, 1964).

This character, The Yellow Claw was a true criminal. His skin was bright yellow in color. He even had an evil appearance and long fingernails. He was constantly thinking up horrible plans. If we try to do a Google image search sometime on "The Yellow Claw" we can see how unrealistic this description really was. But in the context of the times, it was not so surprising. During this time many Westerners did not trust the Chinese. They feared China's power. Perhaps that is what Mao Zedong and his followers wanted to achieve in the beginnings of pre-reform China. Although the authors were not alive when these changes were implemented, it is valuable to understand the stages of this great leader's role in the transformation of the country.

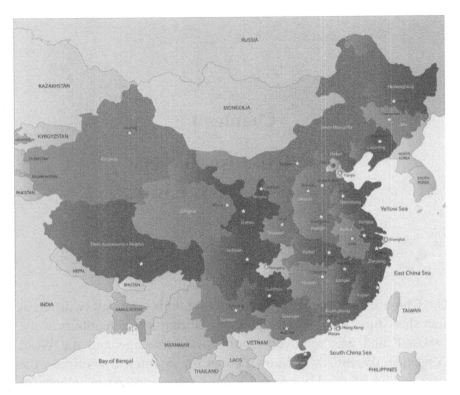

Figure 1: **Map of China is definitely an important tool for us to know more about China's physical landscape and China Studies.**

Under Mao Zedong's leadership in 1949, the Chinese Communist Party (CCP) immediately began a program of revolutionary change. With the changes also came terminology that would become apart of the Chinese system. One of the first mandates was a new marriage law (based on the Soviet model of the 1920s) that set a new course for women and children. From the 1950s to the late 1970s, the central government imposed authoritarian rule and all policies were based on an economy controlled by strict planning guidelines.

In 1958–1961, the regime carried out the Great Leap Forward (大躍進 *Dayuejin*), a radical economic and social campaign aimed at fast-forwarding the country to a prosperous communist society

Photo 1: **In pre-reform China, Buffalo had good utility value to many Chinese since agricultural activities were predominant in society.**

(see Photo 1). It aimed to use China's enormous population to rapidly transform the country from an agrarian economy into a modern Communist society through the process of rapid industrialization and collectivization. The main changes in the lives of rural Chinese included the introduction of a mandatory process of agricultural collectivization.

It abolished private ownership of property and established a new social formation called "the rural people's commune" (人民公社*renmin gongshe*) (see Photos 2, 3, and 4). The Class became heavily conditional on political party affiliation. Property in private hands was confiscated and evenly distributed among every Chinese person.

Private farming was strictly prohibited. Those who engaged in it were labeled as counter-revolutionaries and persecuted. Restrictions

Photo 2:   **In pre-reform China, paddy fields were the major agricultural activities.**

Photo 3:   **Farming was the only and dominant activity in pre-reform China.**

Photo 4:   In pre-reform China, paddy fields were the major agricultural activities.

on rural people were enforced through public struggle sessions and social pressure. Some also experienced forced labor. The Great Leap resulted in millions of deaths. Experts estimate that the death toll ranged from 18 to 32 million people (Cormac, 2011).

In order to maintain strong control over so many people, the CCP, under Mao's direction created social strata that promoted development. The two most prominent social institutions of Maoist China were the *hukou* (戶口 "household registration") and *danwei* (單位 "work unit") systems. To this day, both of these systems continue in modified form in China. The *hukou* system classified the entire population into two categories: agricultural registrants in rural areas and non-agricultural (urban) registrants in metropolitan areas. It was introduced in the 1950s and it quickly became entrenched to the rest of Chinese society by the early 1960s (Tsang, 2014). The *hukou* was a nationwide system of household registration set up under the 1958 Regulations on *Hukou* Registration and issued by the National People's Congress (NPC). It was an effort to safeguard progress towards collectivization in rural areas and to control food shortages in urban China.

The central aim of *hukou* was to regulate internal movement of the Chinese. To accomplish that, it created a legal domicile for every person and bound each person permanently to that dwelling. In other words, the Chinese could not legally move freely around the country. In addition, *hukou* also regulated family daily life. Each family needed to register with the government to maintain family registrations. Because *hukou* was issued for households; it usually included details of births, deaths, marriages, divorces, and movement of all members in the family. Furthermore, the *hukou* also identified a person or household by administrative categories (rural versus urban). It was a system that curtailed geographical mobility of people and also set the tone for an identity of one's native place in China.

The second system that Mao established was *danwei* (Tsang, 2014). The *danwei* system referred to the place of employment, especially in the context of state enterprises during the pre-reform period. The *danwei* was the first step and principal channel for implementing party policy in the Chinese socialist infrastructure. The work unit once held considerable sways on the life of an individual. Workers were bound to their work divisions for life. In some respects, these work units were self-sufficient. Goods and services were provided for including areas of social welfare. These services were provided at the expense of individuals fully complying with government policy. At one time, conditions got so severe that individuals had to obtain permission from their work units for activities such as travel, marriage, childbearing, and even where to have meals. Even areas of job placement for university students were tightly controlled.

With this being said, someone might ask how such a system could be so smoothly enforced. This task was delegated from Mao to cadres. These individuals consisted of government officials with a reasonable amount of power, especially in regulating aspects of everyday life. Political capital or power was central to allowing this group to gain high regard within society.

Still, these seemingly perfect Communistic systems did not always bring the results Mao apparently envisioned. In fact, the years of the Great Leap Forward saw economic regression. One scholar notes that from 1958–1961 there were significantly low financial gains. Excess government spending tended to be the major cause for this issue. Ultimately, The Great Leap was a very expensive disaster for the entire country (Perkins, 1994). This sense of failure and Mao's loss of control within the party brought government leaders to propose even more radical changes to remedy the situation.

Sadly, what resulted was even more devastating. From 1966 to 1976, Mao carried out the Cultural Revolution, a profound campaign to supposedly reroute Chinese society on the fast track to a more socialistic utopia. These changes were designed with the idea that a stronger nation could be build up by removing capitalist, traditional, and cultural elements from society. Of course these changes were replaced by Maoist philosophy. More specifically, the Cultural Revolution was a new effort to correct the mistakes of the Great Leap Forward and to eliminate groups that opposed him. Such groups were consistently characterized as counter-revolutionaries (Chen, 1969).

Many intellectuals, "political subversives" and "educated" youth were sent to remote areas of the country "to learn from the peasants".

Slowly The Cultural Revolution started gaining popularity with just a couple of "big-character posters" on university display boards. This tactic was quickly adopted in other parts of the country. There were many writers and other scholars that were labeled as counter-revolutionaries and brutally attacked. Government sponsored rallies further provoked the minds and hearts of the politically savvy across the country. Broadly speaking, until this point in its history, Maoist China had been a strongly egalitarian, relatively classless yet, impoverished society. With the onset of the revolution the concept

Photo 5:   In post-reform China, it is not hard to find traditional Chinese architectures in downtown Guangdong.

of a middle class was abolished. The Communist Party brought an end to private ownership (capital assets) of property and stripped regional landlords of any power (see Photo 5). Now, political attachment to the party (i.e. political capital) was paramount. This campaign cemented Mao's position of absolute authority. Unfortunately, as part of this "revolution" significant historical relics and artifacts were destroyed. Even cultural sites and religious edifices were ransacked. This era of radicalism would not last for long.

Mao's death in 1976 spring boarded a chain of politico-economic events that softened the extremism that was so popular in the country. It would eventually lead to the opening up of the country to new ideas and systems and pave the way for an economic relationship with the US.

References

Chen, S.Y. (1969). *China: Cultural Revolution or Counter-Revolutionary Coup?* Moscow: Novosti Press Agency Publishing House.

Cormac, Ó.G. (2011). Great Leap into Famine. UCD Centre for Economic Research Working Paper Series. Retrieved on 25 August 2014 from http://www.ucd.ie/t4cms/wp11_03.pdf.

Littlefield, H.M. (1964). The Wizard of Oz: Parable on Populism. *American Quarterly, 16*(1): 47–58.

Perkins, D. (1994). Completing China's Move to the Market. *The Journal of Economic Perspectives, 8*(2): 23–46.

Tsang, E.Y.H. (2014). *The New Middle Class in China, Consumption, Politics and the Market Economy*. London: Palgrave Macmillan.

Chapter 2

The Institutional Changes in Post-Reform China

The Maoist social class structure quickly dissolved since Deng Xiaoping became the chairman in 1980s. He rapidly developed economic growth in China and changed some Maoist social class structures drastically. For examples, Deng tried to develop the Four Modernizations and launched different social and economic reforms since 1980s. From 1978–1992, Deng helped transform China into what became known as a "socialist market economy". Foreign investment, the global market, and limited private competition were acceptable and raised the living standards of millions. For his contributions to humanity, *Time* magazine named him Man of the Year in January 1986 (Time Magazine, 2002). This international magazine's award has since been changed to Person of the Year. Its aim is to feature a person, group, idea or objects that "for better or for worse, has done the most to influence the events of the year" (*Time Magazine*, 2002).

The changing of political ideology was no easy task, not even for the local citizenry. Working class members had to give up their state protected enterprises and communes in exchange for reform. Jobs entailed lifetime employment guaranteed by the state, but adherence to party dogma was still expected. This experience was so commonplace that it became known as the "iron rice bowl" (*tiefanwan* 鐵飯碗) ideology. If a rice bowl made of porcelain falls, it will break on contact, but if the bowl is made of iron, it can drop many times and not be damaged. Thus, this Chinese expression refers to the belief that a government employee could have poor job performance, but make multiple non-party mistakes and not worry about getting fired.

In the beginning, practicality, instead of ideology, drove reform. In 1978, the open-door policy took effect and a new era was beginning in China. The command-and-control limitations in the Chinese economy as well as life in general were modified.

The government replaced the centrally-commanded approach with a more local one. Enterprises and local governments made contracts, which in turn supplied enterprises with production materials and administrative services such as licensing, certification, and tax concessions. Local governments began controlling property rights, resource allocations, and various other bureaucratic processes, including investment and credit resources. Indeed, Deng's mantra of "economics in demand" replaced that of Mao's politics. Even foreign investment was welcomed. Most of the middle class changed from collectively owned enterprise business (*jiti suo you zhi qiye* 集體所有制企業) where assets are collectively owned, to more private ownership. This localization was aided by the creation of Special Economic Zones and dual-track price structures.

Localized Special Economic Zones and foreign joint business ventures accelerated China's economic modernization. In the industrial sector, town and village enterprises (TVEs) developed in coastal regions and cities in Guangdong province, which was the location for our interviews. These TVEs were usually small-scale businesses such as grocery stores and other manufacturing supply companies.

With these new economic areas gaining popularity, financial elements had to also change. Deng Xiaoping implemented the dual-track price structure, where the same commodity was priced differently between the planned and the marketed portions of the economy. Under this system, companies made profit by increasing production of cheaply priced raw materials. Companies made even more profit by pocketing the spread (i.e. price differences) between the state sector and the market. It meant that the Chinese cadres could purchase state produced commodities such as cooking oil, salt, and rice at a cheaper state-controlled price, and sell them at a higher market price to buyers. Cadres often manipulated the incomplete institutional policies for individual profit-taking. It also served as a "breakout" point for the rise of the Chinese new middle class.

Economic liberalization was not the only place for change. Land management also got reworked except for urban land, which remained state-owned. What followed was *land-use rights* only. During the reform years, cadres, and ex-cadres of land-owning work units sold land-use rights at high prices to commercial property companies. The result was a loose but active network of property dealers across different cities increasing the number of land transactions.

The land-leasing system had two main features that emerged from the post-reform era. First, public housing became more privatized and second class became more separate and distinct in China. The *danwei*-based housing philosophy became less desirable and instead a commercial housing model followed in its stead. This process was not equal and thus it created differences in class, especially in urban environments throughout China. Housing was a key factor in the growth of the emerging middle class.

Obviously, private housing is the major factor to determine the socio-economic status in many cosmopolitan cities in post-reform China. Thus, the *hukou* system that Mao established is still to some degree operating in both the urban and rural areas of China. The typical example is the cadre-entrepreneurship which means the former cadre jumped to the sea and become an entrepreneur in 1990s. The allocation of resources continues to be reserved for select groups such as the educated, business tycoons, and government cadres.

These changes have led to an even greater gap between the middle class and other members of society based upon their residence.

The labor force in urban areas of China is about 342 million out of the total 1.4 population (Tsang, 2014). Among the 342 million, approximately 6% are businesspeople and another 6% are professionals (Tsang, 2014). Illegal migrant workers account for almost 12% with a further 12% being unemployed and about 25% forming a "'floating' population". Most of these differences in labor are seen between regions in China, but even large cities such as Beijing, Shanghai and cities in the Special Economic Zone of the Pearl River Delta in Guangdong province are affected. However, it is not easy to make a precise assessment. That is because illegal migrant workers in these cities possess rural *hukou* status and are classified accordingly in official data.

The situation for these illegal workers is unfortunate and well documented. An official report from the Ministry of Labour and Social Security in 2004 found that 68% of all migrant workers in 40 cities across China did not receive one day of rest in the workweek. Worse yet, 76% of workers received no time off for national holidays or *fading jiaqi* (法定假期). With respect to pay, 48% were paid regularly, but 52% experienced occasional and even frequent non-payment of wages, while 54% were never paid overtime earnings (which the law requires employers to do). Concerning employment protection, only one-eighth had employment contracts and only 15% had any social security coverage. The report had other information including overtime payments. The monthly income of illegal migrants was about one quarter that of the 'official' earnings of white-collar workers. However, "legal" manual workers earn only about one third of the monthly earnings of white-collar workers. Clearly, from this data, it can be understood that the new middle class in China has higher salaries and more access to resources, even in excess.

As seen previously, institutional changes have affected several parts of Chinese society. In urban areas, the uneven breakdown of the *danwei* (work unit) system is very common. As we recall, *danwei*, in combination with *hukou*, had been effective in shaping social space and relationships (and therefore identity and class boundaries) for the new middle class in urban China. This has been effective because there are functional and symbolic references of power with *danwei*. But since 1980, the urban *hukou* holder has still been tied to the *danwei* (work unit) from which the individual obtains a wide range of goods and services (Tsang, 2014). Therefore, in urban areas the *danwei* and *hukou* systems combined with *guanxi* (or systems of personal networks) still impact class relations in post-reform China. Traditionally, most of the Chinese new middle class preferred urban *hukou* to a rural one. But beginning in 2010, the Chinese government launched a campaign to attract more people to retain their rural *hukou* by giving more land to the holders of the rural *hukou*. This explains why most of the migrant workers prefer that they preserve their rural *hukou*. Although the urban *hukou* lost its privileges starting in 2010, many urban residents still need their connection with the *danwei* system in order to get the benefits.

Although the *hukou* system might appear restrictive in regards to household registration and lifelong employment, the benefits are many. For example, in urban areas, public housing is regulated by length of service in government posts. Senior employees get better housing accomodations and more options for their children to enjoy the benefits of government work. These two policies and others enable the state to keep adult children dependent on their parents. Even today in China, it appears that urban *hukou* is still very important to the Chinese new middle class, especially for the children of the older generation. These intergeneration transfers *do* bring benefits to their children such as opportunities to study at prestigious primary and secondary schools, and universities. These privileges are less common in the rural *hukou* because of enrollment quotas on students' enrollment.

Professionals and entrepreneurs who are not originally urban *hukou* holders are financially able to afford a *hukou* transfer. This is commonly done through employment with an international company and the payment of cadres. In interviews, members of the new middle class confirmed that they have paid as much as RMB100,000 (US$14,631 or £10,004)[1] to "acquire" an urban *hukou*. Therefore, the most distinguishing feature of a member of the Chinese new middle class is having an urban *hukou* as opposed to one who does not, usually the peasant.

These economic reforms and thriving commerce have caused many professionals, entrepreneurs, and cadres to move into the newly established industrial and development zones predominantly located in Guangdong province. The rapidly growing economy since the 1990s paved the way and offered a good chance for the cadres who worked in the state owned enterprises (SOEs) to make the switch to doing business with private companies (*xiahai* 下海 "to dive into the sea", it means doing business and become an entrepreneur).

The privileged position associated with the urban Chinese new middle class became progressively prominent throughout the reform years and it appears that will be the case in the future as well (Shanghai Education Department, 2012). The *guanxi* circles that ex-state workers developed during their tenure with their *danwei* remain useable and important even after their switch to the business world.

The New China is operating under "socialism with Chinese characteristics" albeit capitalism with a pseudonym. This government structure focuses on relationships and connections with people of power. Common activities include gift-giving, wining and dining, collective memories, traditional Chinese values, and the need for self-improvement. The relationship-oriented nature of Chinese society allows the society to operate and encourages *guanxi* networks (Zhang, 1999).

---

[1] All Exchange Rates Used in this Study are RMB1 = US$0.146 and RMB1 = £0.102 Mid-Market Spot Rates. Retrieved on 25 May 2010 from www.xe.com on.

Guanxi is probably the single biggest factor that stimulates economic growth in China (Chen, 1994). Even the "upper class" in present-day China is closely intertwined with kinship networks. Many of these wealthy ex-cadres, for example, who have strong ties and close affiliations with the government, use the *guanxi* or network system within class boundaries to build up wealth. The cadre-dominated social hierarchy still exists as a result of the household registration system from the late 1950s. Many businesspeople and professionals consider cadres as the tiebreakers (*jueshengfu* 決勝負) in issuing those business licenses, and are thus in positions needed of respect. During the course of a cadre's official duties, gift giving and receiving is routine. This is an almost universal situation in the Guangdong region of China (see Photo 1). Westerners might view this as bribery, but the Chinese see it differently. Chinese culture values social honor, sensibility and "face" (Hwang, 2010). This is illustrated when employees compare gift money from celebrations or even funerals to show which person has more face than others.

Photo 1: In downtown Guangdong, it is not difficult to find business and commercial settings.

Thus, *guanxi* networks are increasingly important to get ahead in post-reform China as the country becomes more capitalistic.

Commercial reforms in China have brought a greater degree of prosperity for many across China. Both institutional changes and longstanding interpersonal networks of *guanxi* have created a seemingly hybrid version of governance. The emergence of the Chinese new middle class illustrates the importance of "class". Class consists of factors such as education, market, political values, and the ruling party in the country. In looking at the rising new middle class in transitional China today, it is clear the Chinese economic situation can be classified as "socialism with Chinese characteristics".

References

Chen, M. (1994). Guanxi and the Chinese Art of Network Building. *New Asia Review*, Summer, 40–43.

Hwang, K.K. (2010). Face and Favor: The Chinese Power Game. *American Journal of Sociology*, 92(4): 944–974.

Shanghai Education Department, (2012). Future Education in China (In Chinese). Retrieved on 25 June 2012 from http://www.chinadetail.com/Nation/CityGovernmentShanghai.php.

Time Magazine (2002). *Person of the Year: 75th Anniversary Celebration.* New York: Time Books, 1–10.

Tsang, E.Y.H. (2014). *The New Middle Class in China, Consumption, Politics and the Market Economy*, London: Palgrave Macmillan, 10–15.

Zhang, W.G. (1999). Implementation of State Family Planning Programmes in a Northern Chinese Village. *China Quarterly, 157*: 202–230.

Part II
Socio-Economic Changes in the Chinese Societies

Chapter 3

Chinese Family and Kinship: Yesterday and Today

The traditional family in China consisted of parents, children, extended family, and even kinship relationships. Under this pre-reform China model, male children were especially important in rural areas due to the need for labor on farms. The word "family" usually referred to a married couple who may or may not have children. There were at least three different types of families: simple, stem, and extended family. The sociologist Hugh (1979)[1] pinpointed that family in traditional China was a residential and economic unit composed of males. In both pre- and post-reform China, society is usually dominated by males. In the following chapter we will discuss the changes in the post-reform Chinese family and its implications today.

When we think of China, one of the first things to pop into our head is the one child situation. We might be familiar with it or read about it in a magazine. Although it is highly misunderstood, it has created numerous social repercussions not only in China, but even the

---

[1] Huge, B.D.R. (1979). *Chinese Family and Kinship*. New York: Columbia University Press, p. 17.

world. The One Child Policy began in 1978 as a way to address over-population concerns across the country. This is a government mandate (not an economic decision like in the US), which states that parents shall have only one child per household. Today, families violating the policy are required to pay hefty fines as high as RMB453,000 (US$12,000 or £6,000). In urban areas the policy has been strongly enforced, but its actual implementation varies across the country.

The policy is modified slightly in rural areas of China. Here, families are allowed to apply to have a second child if the first is a girl, or has a physical disability, mental illness, or mental retardation. If someone tries to choose to have additional children will result in large fines. Some villagers have protested against such policies and heavy fines by burning cars, damaging buildings, and fighting with police, but not much success. Worse yet, women have reported cases of being forced to have abortions for exceeding the child quota. Sometimes, government sanctions can be severe. Many children were put up for foreign adoption in a poverty stricken region of Hunan province in the south of the country. This was the result of parents breaking the One Child Policy (Worldcrunch Report).

Another adaptation to the policy states that Hong Kong and Macau citizens do not need to abide by the policy. Also, children born overseas are not considered in the policy if they do not obtain Chinese citizenship. Some families have evaded the system by giving birth in another province and then "hiding" children in the homes of different relatives over a period of time. To avoid suspicion, they often refer to their additional child as a "cousin". This exception is commonly referred to as "birth tourism". Finally, Chinese citizens returning from abroad can have a second child. Some families are wealthy enough that they can have as many children as they like and afford to pay fines. These are certainly exceptions to the policy and not the norm.

Another strategy used by some mainland Chinese women is to give birth to their second child out of the country. A popular destination is Hong Kong, the US, or other part in Europe. In 2010, the

Hong Kong government reported that about 45% of its country's births were such women. Not only is Hong Kong exempt from the One-Child Policy, but also the Hong Kong passport is different from the mainland's passport. This provides additional advantages including free public education, political freedom and ease of worldwide travel. However, the so-called anchor baby issue intensifies and deteriorates the Hong Kong–China relationship. On first February 2012, a giant locust hovering over Hong Kong's picturesque skyline featured as a full-paged advertisement in the *Apple Daily* (15 April 2014); a popular local newspaper. A commentary besides the locust enumerated the estimated financial cost Hong Kong taxpayers would have to bear for hosting each "locust" "shuangfei child 雙非嬰兒" (i.e. a child without at least one being a Hong Kong citizen) in their territory. In Hong Kong, the "locust" (*huangchong* 蝗蟲) is a derogatory term used to castigate immigrants and tourists from mainland China (hereafter "Mainlanders") as their culturally inferior and imperilling "unequal others" culpable for denuding Hong Kong's social welfare resources. This advertisement was unequivocal in calling for a timely end to the unlimited infiltration of mainland Chinese couples into Hong Kong society. It is noteworthy that this advertisement was funded by the proceeds of a spontaneous online fund-raising campaign on Facebook, a well-known social networking website in conjunction with a local online group, the Golden Forum, which received more than 100,000 Hong Kong dollars (US$12,900) from 800 donors within a week.

This influx of baby deliveries in Hong Kong has created a new baby business. It can be equated to a baby delivery travel agency. Such companies help Chinese women go to Hong Kong to give birth. The agency fees can be very costly, as high as thousands of US dollars. Now, the Health Authority in Hong Kong has instituted quotas for non-local residents. Those quotas apply to both public and private hospitals. In addition, the Hong Kong government has also prosecuted agencies that violate immigration laws as part of this birthing process. Hong Kong's new Chief Executive, Leung

Chun-Ying, wants to go even further and put a stop to the practice entirely. He feels mainland Chinese mothers should be banned from private hospitals and that the laws should be changed so that their newborns will no longer be able to claim permanent residence. However, Hong Kong's new leader has not offered any specifics as to how he hopes to accomplish that goal.

Another popular location that is close to China is Saipan on the Northern Mariana Islands. This island is a US dependency in the western Pacific Ocean and permits Chinese to visit freely without visa restrictions. This has caused the island to see an increase in the number of births.

Still some wealthy Chinese set their sights beyond Hong Kong and the Pacific as the birthplace for their children. Mainland agencies also offer arrangements for going to North America. The US has a practice of birthright citizenship, meaning that children born in the US *will* be US citizens. Canada is another alternative, but in recent years, not as popular since the country typically denies visa requests.

Whatever options these wealthy Chinese choose, they might be thinking about the long-term for their family as well. Parents might want their children to be able to leave Communist China when they grow older or bring their parents to their new home abroad. Regardless, every decision those families are making impacts something else. As a result of the large scale of migration within families, society as a whole is also being affected.

While the post-reform aim of the One Child Policy was originally to curb overpopulation, it is simultaneously affecting other areas of the family unit, such as care for the elderly. In China, children are expected to support and provide for the care of their parents and grandparents. We can only imagine how this situation gets troublesome for a single child, even in adult years, trying to care for needy grandparents. This predicament is so popular in China that it is called the "4-2-1 problem"[2] (Wen, 2008). In serious events of

---

[2] 4-2-1 means only the young generation will have to bear the responsibility of supporting both of their parents and grandparents.

money failures or loss of pensions, the responsibility of care of the family member would the small immediate family unit. This situation is on the rise throughout China's young adult population. Many young people today work in factories, which subsidize much of their living expenses but they do not earn a high enough salary to support their extended family members. The government has intervened and some provinces allow single child parents to have two children in hope to remedy this catastrophe.

Another issue facing China's family of today is that of gender imbalance that the One Child Policy has created. The National Population and Family Planning Commission reported that by 2020 there will be 30 million more men than women in China. Thus there is a high demand for females but a low supply. As stated previously, Chinese society has traditionally favored males and it seems that some families may be engaging in their own form of family planning. *The Times* of London reports that many Chinese have aborted female fetuses. Abortion is legal and widely available in China. But the country *does* prohibit tests to determine the gender of a fetus for non-medical reasons. *The Times* finds that female infanticide is widespread, but rarely mentioned.

As we can see, China's One Child Policy is creating both short and long-term issues. But what about the larger picture of Chinese society? Are the traditional family values still able to survive in a changing society? Perhaps there are some modifications. Just like in the US, many women are no longer stay-at-home mothers and someone else needs to care for the child. That is where the grandparents enter the picture.

Throughout China it is common to see children and babies with older individuals. This is because the grandparents are tending to the childrearing while the parents are at work (see Photo 1).

In the US and other European countries, daycare is quite popular. But in China such commercial centers are replaced by grandma and grandpa. Depending upon the socio-economic status of the family, access to and care of one's child differs. In wealthier families,

Photo 1:   The grandparent takes care of the Asian babies. They have special baby carriers made by bamboo basket.

grandparents watch after the child while the parents are working. In lower income families, parents usually live and work in different cities than that of the grandparents. Thus, during the workweek, the grandparents tend to the child and only on weekends the parents are able to see their children. Many of these aforementioned families are migrant workers who only return home once or twice a year. Children raised under such circumstances are referred to as "left-behind children" (Stack, 2010).

Despite these changes in the family unit across China, Chinese Lunar New Year provides an opportunity to reconnect. For migrant workers it may be the *only* time they are able to visit their home-town all year long. For others, a busy lifestyle may mean it is a chance to spend extra time with family during holiday time. Regardless of economic status, family still plays an important role in Chinese culture.

A final element that differentiates China of today with the China of yesterday is the role of women in the family. With more women in the work force, it also means less time dedicated to childrearing. A married woman becomes an equal partner in the family income. In fact, in some families today, professional wives earn a higher salary than their husbands (Department of Economic and Social Affairs, 2010). This is indeed a departure from Chinese tradition in which men dominated society. This is a drastic change from times when women had no rights or privileges. The opening up of China to the US, which started in the 1970s, laid the groundwork for the economic changes, which ultimately helped change the role of women. Furthermore, Mao Zedong's contribution when he took control of China in 1949 was the promotion of gender equality. He instituted policies to eliminate the oppression of women and although not always enforced they *were* still the rules under Maoist China. Women were given equal opportunities in both the job market and education and developed many new ways of conduct that were traditionally not part of Chinese culture (China party, 2005). This included the freedom to choose one's own husband. New marriage laws outlawed arranged marriages. Prior to this time, the selection of a marriage partner was a family affair instead of the individual and males could have a concubine.

Even as late as the 20th century, it was considered acceptable for a man to have more than one wife, especially if the first wife did not produce male offspring. It was acceptable as long as the family finances could handle it. Sociologists report secondary wives still exist, although today they are often kept a secret, sometimes in a different country. Some wealthy businessmen from Hong Kong are believed to engage in this practice during their travels between the mainland and the island.

Some additional changes that women experience in China include wives being given equal rights with their husbands in managing family property, increased educational opportunites, more

Photo 2:   Marriage is an important milestone for women, Chinese women are not an exception.

voice in family decisions, and higher managerial positions (see Photo 2). With these changes in the lives of women, they are still expected to uphold typical tradtional roles of women such as nurturing and caring for children, which can be an added burden.

Although there were some aspects of early Mao communism that betrayed the family unit, especially during the Cultural Revolution, the later reform era of Deng Xiaoping, reinstituted traditional family values back into society. It was also a period when traditions abandoned out of fear of reprisal were revived. The New China is a culture that is attempting to mesh traditional values such as strong care for the elderly and strong family times despite changing job demands. The New China requires new solutions to lessen the repercussions of the One Child Policy and social issues that insured.

References

China Daily (6 December 2005). First Book on Rural Enterprises, *Xinhuanet.* Retrieved on 9 September 2008 from http://news.xinhuanet.com/english/2005-12/06/content_3883231.htm.

Department of Economic and Social Affairs (2010). The World's Women 2010-Trend and Statistics United Nations. Retrieved on 10 August 2014 from http://unstats.un.org/unsd/demographic/products/Worldswomen/WW_full%20report_color.pdf.

Stack, M.K. (29 September 2010). China Raising a Generation of Left-Behind Children. *Los Angeles Times.* Retrieved 25 August 2014 from http://articles.latimes.com/2010/sep/29/world/la-fg-china-left-behind-20100930.

Wen, L. (5 April 2008). Four-Two-One Families', Where Is the Road Going? Yunnan Daily Online. Retrieved on 31 December 2014 from http://en.people.cn/102775/208085/index.html.

Worldcrunch Report. Retrieved on 13 January 2015 from http://www.worldcrunch.com/.

Chapter 4

Chinese Women and Education: Better Off in Post-Socialist China?

When I was teaching at one University in Guangdong, China, I noticed that a large percentage of students were female. About 70% of the entire student body was comprised of women. From a global perspective this might not be such a significant statistic, but in the Chinese cultural context, this is a significant change. In the previous chapter we mentioned the changing role of women in Chinese society. In this chapter we will further explore this issue.

Many parents today across China are willing to invest in the education of their female children. Traditionally, families would combine their resources in support of men, instead of women as per Confucian beliefs. Women were considered "lost" and usually confined to degrading, low-end jobs. Many viewed a daughter's role as chef and house cleaner; until she got married at which time she became the property of her husband's family.

Confucius further professed a philosophy of ways in which women should conduct themselves in greater society and in the home. On both micro and macro levels women were expected to be subservient to men and their husbands. Below are some adages by Confucius that illustrate this thinking.

(1) A woman should look upon her husband as if he were Heaven itself, and never worry of thinking how she may yield to him.
(2) Women are to be led and to follow others.
(3) We should not be too familiar with the lower orders or with women.
(4) A woman's duty is not to control or take charge.

Such cultural values have been engrained into the hearts and minds of Chinese for centuries, which make change seemingly slow and unnoticeable. But when the Communist Party came to power, one of its main priorities was equality between men and women. Education was a fundamental element of government decrees which aimed to raise the status of women. It remains to be seen whether members of society truly embraced such changes and had positive attitudes toward such changes. In 1959, the *China Statistical Yearbook* reported that as much as 90% of women in China were illiterate. As Communist China had done in the past, it launched a campaign to change this. The government provided day and night literacy classes for women in both urban and rural areas. From these concerted efforts, the government claimed in 1970 that there were 16 million women who had learned to read (*China Statistical Yearbook*, 1971). This was certainly a start in changing the status of Chinese women.

Education was not the only area that contributed to advancement of women's rights in China. In 1953, an Electoral Law took effect and allowed women the same rights to vote in elections as men. During this period women began making their way into the work force and could earn an independent income. In the past, it was common to note that women played a key role in the development of Chinatowns around the world in the early 20th Century because of their ability to obtain higher education and work experience abroad. Certainly this was novel behavior for women of this time period to expand the cultural envelope and it paved the way for society's acceptance toward other government policies in China.

With the onset of China's One Child Policy, and other social factors many Chinese are rethinking and to some degree questioning such long held Confucian beliefs. For example, many young women are postponing marriage possibly because of the disconnected feeling that it is their "duty" to find a partner. Also, the concern for caring for parents, finding the "right" partner, and pursuing higher education are understandably daunting tasks for women today.

I witnessed such familial concerns during my fieldwork research with new middle class families and individuals in China. I noticed that the parents were arguing over their daughter's major at university and considered which major would land her a better career. From both the parent and daughter perspectives, the topic had high consequences and high emotions. Regardless of the parent's level, I noticed that the parents still did not fully understand the changing nature of the job market even in modern China.

Education has become a form of consumption. And like any other consumption item, educational consumption often is based on one's economic capability and intelligence. Excellent educational resources . . . are scarce and should be priced at a higher level. It is natural that not everyone can afford excellent educational resources. It is like shopping for clothing. A well-off man can go to a brand-name store to buy a 10,000 yuan suit, while a poor person can buy a 100-yuan suit from a vendor (Wang, 2006). Many parents were troubled by their daughters' educational prospects. Fong, a 48-year-old entrepreneur, shared her feelings toward supporting her daughter's education:

> I don't care how much I spend on my kid's education, I just want her to study at the brand-name university and get a relatively stable job either in the USA or China. I will try my best to facilitate my *guanxi* to help her to get a job in China. It really depends where will she stay. If she wants to come back to China, I have already prepared lots of jobs for her.

With educational pursuits being at the forefront of women's minds, this mentality can also affect women's marriage prospects. Some men might feel intimidated because their wives have a higher salary or there are less eligible males with similar education level. This has led to some Chinese women seeking foreign marriage partners.[1] Clearly this gives today's women in China more options and autonomy from traditional norms including liberalized divorce laws which might deter women from marrying for fear of being another statistic.

Descendants of the affluent Chinese middle class, collectively known as the second-generation middle class, comprise the majority of students in most of China's private universities. The increasingly globalized nature of the media, their familiarity with the English language, and growing opportunities for higher education in Anglophone countries have lured them to private universities in China. The quotation above fully depicts the perceived social role of education in today's China.[2] The expansion of transnational higher education in China, which evolves from "cooperation between foreign education institutions and Chinese education institutions in China, catering for the needs of Chinese citizens" (State Council of China, 2003), is not only an expression of the transitional Chinese community's mode of existence, but also a part of a community composed of ambitious, well-educated middle-class people who are anxious to cement their social status in post-reform China (Fong, 2004; Fang, 2012). This coincides with the emergence of private universities since the 1990s which has been encouraged and supported by the central government in an attempt to shift the

---

[1] More details see chinawhisper.com. Retrieved on 12 September 2014.

[2] For example, in the UK, an overseas student needs to pay an average of £16,000 (US$25,000) a year for boarding-school education — about 10 times the average annual income of an urban Chinese household in 2003. Meanwhile, about 7,000 students from China study in Australia at secondary level each year, accounting for half of the students studying abroad on student visas in 2003. The number of students abroad is growing by 10% a year (Economist, 2003). China's princelings are going abroad for their schooling. March 27.

financial burden of expanding higher education from the state. There are 37 Sino-foreign higher education institutions in China and the majority of them are located in the more affluent coastal provinces or municipalities such as Shanghai, Liaoning, Beijing, Shandong, Jiangsu, and Guangdong (Chinese Ministry of Education, 2013). There are more well educated females received their higher education in private universities as well as transnational higher education institutes than men in today's China (Tsang, 2014).

In a 2005 Chinese government "white paper" it cited that women not only have active roles in education but they also contribute to its betterment (State Council, White Paper). In 1990, 50,000 teachers were cited for having made outstanding contributions. Around 70% of them were women. Additionally, in 1993, 5,971 people were cited as exemplary teachers and education workers in the national education system, among them 1,702 being women, or 28.5% of the total. Over 20 women across the country assume the posts of university President or Vice President (State Council, White Paper). In one of China's most prestigious universities, Beijing University alone, almost one-third of the 3,000 academics are female. Among them, 19 are tutors of postgraduate candidates, 68 are professors, and more than 300 are associate professors. Indeed, women are actively contributing to education across China[3] (State Council, White Paper, 2005).

With so many accomplishments and strides forward, there still remains an obstacle for women. There are hurdles both in rural and urban areas alike; no one is exempt. For example, school admission standards for men and women are not equal. Senior high school female students must score 10 to 20 points higher on entrance exams than the minimum required of male students. Furthermore, sociologists wonder if the gains for women in China have been as

---

[3] The State Council Information Office, (2005). *Gender Equality and Women's Development in China.* Beijing: State Council. Retrieved from http://www.china.org.cn/english/2005/Aug/139404.htm.

pronounced as they appear to be and recent government reforms appear to have brought mixed results.

Many women from rural areas of China are trying to move to urban centers and find new opportunities. But in the current system, they do not have residency permits and are eventually denied medical and educational benefits for their children. Additionally, mothers in this situation must pay higher school fees than local urban residents. Another option such mothers have is to matriculate their children in cheap private migrant schools, which are not legally recognized. This leaves many mothers with difficult decisions regarding the education.

Just as Women's roles in China have changed a lot in post-reform China, so also has the educational system in China in light of post-Socialism government, reforms. China's Ministry of Education allocates funding based upon regions with branches at provincial and local levels. This hierarchy affects the quality of the education for children and with such a large student population, resources are limited. This situation is made worse by the decentralization policy from the central government because there is less state funding, which places a greater responsibility on local governments. In turn, many local governments have delegated the task of school funding to the schools themselves.

These changes of administration in education have caused tuition fees to increase. The Standard of the Shanghai Education Department,[4] reported that the tuition fees are as follows: 14,000 yuan (US$1,866/£1,271) for three years of kindergarten, 15,000 yuan (US$2,450/£1,363) for five years of primary school, 30,000 yuan (US$4,000/£2,727) for seven years of secondary school, and 46,000 yuan (US$7,516/£4,181) for four years of college. This means that in order for a family to send one child through the complete

---

[4] Shanghai Education Department, (2012). *Future Education in China* (In Chinese). Retrieved from http://www.chinadetail.com/Nation/CityGovernment Shanghai.php. Retrieved on 12 May 2014.

education system (kindergarten to university) in China, parents must pay a total of 105,000 yuan (US$17,156/£9,545) in tuition fees alone, excluding daily living expenses (Shanghai Education Department, 2012). For many average and middle class Chinese families this is great burden. This stress may be reflect by recent data indicating increasing school dropout rates.

Worse yet, because many parents in the countryside have exceptions to the One Child Policy and can have a son and a daughter, most parents prefer to make educational investments in their sons. It is clear that the expensive compulsory tuition fee is also negatively impacting women's education.

One might wonder if there is any solution to this educational problem. One possible resolution is school-run businesses. This is a unique characteristic of China's education system, in which the government encourages schools to opt in and gives businesses special treatment, such as tax exemptions. Those businesses include textile, farming, fishing, and printing industries. About 93% of all Chinese primary and secondary schools have school-run businesses. In the decade prior to 2001, the school-run businesses across the nation had net incomes of about 40 billion yuan (about US$5 billion) in which 55.38% of these were invested in education (Shanghai Education Department, 2012). Such businesses are more widespread in rural parts of China.

The down side of these business ventures is that students must have "practical training", meaning students perform physical labor in order to get their education. This practice is extremely popular in rural area schools where children must work in dangerous industries including mines and livestock farms. One tragic example of this was when 50 children and four adults were killed in a rural area near Dongguan while assembling fireworks in their classroom. They were working for a local business to collect funds for the school. Despite the international disapproval of this event, such activities still continue across China. Incidents such as this only add to the division between rich and poor.

Until the turn of the 21st century, most Chinese students studied at state-run universities or colleges and relied on government scholarships for studying abroad. Foreign educational institutions then began to show great interest in investing in higher education in China (Ennew and Yang, 2009). Around 200 British institutions offer various study programs in China, with some 11,000 students pursuing joint Chinese–British academic degrees under such programs. American academic institutions, including Duke University, New York University, Columbia University, and many others colleges, are also active in collaborating with Chinese educational institutions. It is estimated that well over 1,000 foreign academic institutions have expressed keen interests in establishing private universities in China (Fazackerley, 2007). This development is in synchronization with the emergence of a new middle class, one of the drastic social changes in China over the past 30 years or so, especially in the southern province of Guangdong which enjoys an average annual economic growth rate of approximately 10%.

Families with more wealth and disposable income can afford to send their children to a private school for compulsory education. When the child is ready to attend university, many American higher education institutions are elated to accept such wealthy students simply because schools do not need to supply them with scholarships. Furthermore, Chinese international students pay "out of state" tuition rates that are much higher than local US citizens. This practice is so common that the US Consulate General supplies many online resources for assisting students who pursue such an educational track.

Women's roles in China and the education situation they experience have certainly changed in light of post-socialist politics. Still one's family financial situation and location (whether rural or urban) affect the benefits that one receives. An area of great concern remains in the disparity of resources in urban and rural areas. Indeed there is much to be done to improve China's education system. Depending upon how the Chinese government chooses to address the issue of education will directly impact many women and their future development.

References

China Statistical Yearbook (1971). Retrieved on 12 January 2015 from http://tongji.cnki.net/kns55/navi/HomePage.aspx?id=N2013110049 &name=YINFN&floor=1.

Chinese Ministry of Education (2013). Chinese-Foreign Cooperation in Running Schools. Retrieved on 5 February 2013 from http://www.crs.jsj.edu.cn/index.php/default/approval/getbyarea/1.

Ennew, C.T. & Yang, F. (2009). Foreign Universities in China: A Case Study. *European Journal of Education*, *44*(1): 21–36.

Fang, W. (2012). The Development of Transnational Higher Education in China: A Comparative Study of Research Universities and Teaching Universities. *Journal of Studies in International Education*, *16*(1): 5–23.

Fazackerley, A. & Worthington (2007). *British Universities in China*. London: Agora: The Forum for Culture and Education.

Fong, (2004), Filial Nationalism among Chinese Teenagers with Global Identities. Vanessa Fong. *American Ethnologist*, *31*(4): 629–646.

State Council of China (2003). *Regulations of the People's Republic of China on ZhongwaiHezuo Banxue*. Retrieved on 10 December 2013 from http://www.gov.cn/gongbao/content/2003/content_62030.htm.

State Council, White Paper (2005). The State Council Information Office. *Gender Equality and Women's Development in China*. Beijing: State Council. Retrieved from http://www.china.org.cn/english/2005/Aug/139404.htm. Retrieved on 12 May 2014

Tsang, Y.H. (2014). *The New Middle Class in China*: *Consumption, Politics and the Market Economy*. London: Palgrave Macillian.

Wang, X. (2006). China Ministry of Education Spokesperson. *Beijing Review,* 30: 21–22.

Chapter 5

Emergence
of the Chinese New Middle Class

Thanks to mass media, especially television, many people all over the World have seen glimpses of what Chinese society looks like. This was best exemplified by the 2008 Beijing Olympics. People in the US saw China's modern capital city and other parts of the country. Yet, if you were to ask an average foreigner, American for example, to describe China, they might allude to a poor farmer standing in a rice paddy with a dirty water buffalo. True, this is a common occurrence in China, but it certainly does not describe all of China's new middle class. Back in 1992, Chinese leader Deng Xiaoping uttered his famous phrase 'to get rich is glorious'. It seems the Chinese new middle class decided to be part of that prophesy in a big way. So who exactly belongs to this new Chinese middle class and how is it defined? The framework for this question is drawn from in-depth longitudinal in-depth interviews from 2001 to 2009 in Guangdong province, China. Certainly, in the changing cultural landscape of post-reform China, this definition is subject to change.

Defining the Chinese New Middle Class

There is no widely held definition of the middle class among Chinese sociologists who are more inclined to use income, occupation, education, and consumption as the key criteria for classification. Similarly, Li and Zhang identified China's middle class by measures of middle-level urban household income, white-collar occupations, and higher-education qualifications. Up to 26% of these total populations meet at least one of these criteria, while only 3.2% fulfill all three conditions and are designated as the "core middle class". Another study focuses narrowly on "educated salaried professionals" whose "superior market situation ... is mostly derived from their higher education credentials, professional expertise, and authoritative position rather than from their ownership of private property". In Western sociology, the middle class is a slippery concept too, although it may be broadly defined as a group of people who have non-manual occupations. Possessing property, organizational and cultural assets (or three "class assets") respectively, the petite bourgeoisie, managers and professional workers can be considered members of the middle class.

Most of the Chinese new middle class have and inherit urban *hukou* and are closely connected with each other via their previous *danwei*. They befriend with and trust each other because they share similar cultural practices and dispositions, and lifestyles. As shown next, most members of the middle class under the scrutiny of this study have grown out of and benefited from the socialist institutions of *danwei*, (urban) *hukou*, and *guanxi* under a more market-friendly environment. The interpersonal, particularistic ties developed in such a social context can be regarded as the resources (or social capital, as discussed in more detail next) whereby one uses to gain advantages (Bian, 2001; Portes, 1998). Their social significance is not in demise, even under economic reforms, because Chinese entrepreneurs, professionals, and cadres are unlikely able to espouse common class-consciousness to uphold common actions to safeguard their common interests, as shown in public discourse that downplays the legitimacy and role of class (Guo, 2012). They instead tend to have and exhibit a common *habitus* featuring cultural and economic display of extravagant living (Gerth, 2011; Goodman, 2014). Partly because of these, it is unlikely that they can maintain a common identity and a class-wide network (Ma & Cheng, 2010). Rather they are inclined to sustain personal, particularistic ties with each other to procure particularistic privileges (Guo & Miller, 2010). In short, entrepreneurs, professionals, and cadres pursue interests competitively through personal networks rather than acting collectively to acquire and share collective benefits.

Drawing on Bourdieu's cultural studies of class, which argued that classes can be distinguished in accordance by the types and amount of capital people possess, we conceptualize the Chinese middle class as the one composed of those who possess varying amount of economic capital, cultural capital, or social capital. Prominent examples are private entrepreneurs, party-state cadres, state-owned enterprise managers, and professionals such as lawyers, media personalities, and intellectuals working in universities. Most members of the middle class in this study have grown out of and benefited from the Maoist socialist institutions of urban *danwei*, urban *hukou*, and *guanxi* under a more market-friendly environment. Both urban *hukou* and *danwei* create the social context for cadre-centered *guanxi* networks, which facilitate the expansion of the new middle class, to continue to prosper.

Conspicuous Consumption

Consumption has been studied by students of marketing and sociology. Whereas students of marketing are interested in what affects consumers' choices of goods (see, e.g. Amaldoss & Jain, 2005; Podoshen *et al.*, 2011), sociologists are concerned with social standing and distinctions expressed through consumption. They argue that the goods and services bought by status-seeking consumers, notably a group known as *nouveaux* riches, are often intended to show others in a visible manner what their social standing in a status hierarchy is or what they aspire it to be. By embodying taste, consumption is a marker of social class. Consumer goods are valued as symbols of status, which, in turn, determines consumers' differential access to scarce and valued resources. To put it differently, consumption produces and reproduces social inequality.

Veblen's *The Theory of the Leisure Class* (1899/1934) was the first that provided insight into the relationship between consumption and class. He stated that material factors determine cultural consumption, and the purpose of cultural practices is to demonstrate and display material status. The affluent also consume society's scarce cultural resources. Thus, people with money are deemed to have culture, while impoverished people are, by definition, uncultured. For Veblen, conspicuous leisure and consumption demonstrate one's "distance from mundane, productive labor". To attract public admiration, the affluent leisure class would consume goods in wasteful and highly visible manners. That means consumers do not buy things for reasons of utility, functionality or actual needs, but rather for the images associated with what are consumed — i.e. consumer items (both goods and services) are pure signs (acting as signifiers). In short, conspicuous consumption is a type of hedonist behavior in which an individual displays wealth ostentatiously through a lifestyle of luxury in order to earn social admiration and emulation (Trigg, 2001).

On many streets in and around Guangdong province's cities and villages, it is easy to experience the same mood as the hustle and bustle of Hong Kong. There are many of the same chain stores and outlets such as G2000, McDonald's, Starbucks, Park'n Shop, Chow Tai Fook Jewellers, as well as other well-known Hong Kong brandnames. In fact, Shenzhen, Dongguan, Zhuhai, Guangzhou, Zhongshan, and even more obscure cities like Yangjiang now appear more like modern, cosmopolitan cities. Although Guangdong province is relatively young when compared with other provinces in China, it still has its own unique historical and economic characteristics. Guangdong's GNP per capita was 6,779,224 millions in 2014 (China NBS — National Data, 2015).

Whether taking public transport, high-speed rail, or simply walking through the cities of Guangdong province, it is easy to find advertising on billboards with fashionable models showing off new products and apparel. Advertising is everywhere. In a relatively short time, China has turned into a marketing wonderland for international brands, which are looking for consumers like the Chinese new middle class to promote their profits. A quick stroll along Dongmen Walk in Shenzhen is representative of the growing cosmopolitan nature that has come to characterize many parts of Guangdong.

With shopping malls, skyscrapers, restaurants, and pop music, this part of China is becoming very much like any other modern Western city. Guangzhou and Shenzhen, two major cities in Guangdong province, boast the highest per-capita income of the province. There are many noticeable signs of consumption amongst the young generation, especially brand-name products, latest versions of mobile phones, and big-name cars. These two cities have vast wealth, which is why prestigious retailers such as Louis Vuitton S.A. and luxury department stores Lane Crawford, Prada, and other brand names have moved in.

Many individuals in management positions of large companies value their "dress code" of Guccis and Rolexes. This supposedly presents a more professional image to others. Dress codes are often obvious identifiers of the new middle class's social status. This strategy also helps to develop or increase business partners. Conspicuous consumption is important for the young generation because they often lack well-developed networks or business associates. The ability to consume conspicuously enables them to impress others. They believe it gives them the capability to take on major business undertakings.

In many parts of Guangdong province, consumption is no longer just about buying tangible things such as clothing and accessories. It has also spread to buying services that improve living standards. Thus, hiring babysitters, chauffeurs, family doctors, travel consultants, financial planners, insurance agents, stockbrokers, and much more has become very popular.

Rising Consumption of Branded Goods

The rising consumption of branded goods has rapidly swept through Guangdong since the economic reform. The young generation tends to be more fashionable, stylish, and concerned with image. The beauty care industry in China is very profitable and allows the young middle class to capitalize on their bodies. Consumption in this area is more associated with status symbols and by buying brand-name products many feel a sense of superiority in an increasingly free and open market of life changes (see Photo 1).

Photo 1: Luxury brand names are common in Guangdong province, China.

Indeed it appears that the purpose is to flaunt their wealth and status. The mantra of many of the young generations is to purchase conspicuous "mansions" and luxury cars to make them stand out. They continuously exhibit lavish spending behavior in the form of expensive merchandise and luxury services that allows them to showcase their financial power and higher status in society. They dine at luxury restaurants, place high-priced bids on auspicious-sounding mobile phone numbers or car number plates, set up extravagant banquets, and travel.

Generally speaking, the young generation is a prime consumer target for retailers and service providers in China because of their relatively high purchasing power compared to the rest of the population. Their power tends to be driven by the pleasure-seeking principle of hedonism and a need to be seen by others as modern and up-to-date. Lily, a 30-year-old professional describes her personal experience[1]:

> I am addicted and really like to buy brand names like LV, Porter, Agnes b, Polo, and Vivienne Westwood. I'll buy it from Hong Kong but not from China. I don't want others to think I'm using counterfeits. I like these brands because they make me feel different from other people. Perhaps these brand names are expensive to buy. Sometimes, I accompany my mother and my husband (who is an assistant professor in Hong Kong) to go to Europe, Paris and Japan to buy these brand names (Lily, 30, Professional).

The rising consumption of brand-name goods in China is not just a quantitative change, but it is also an expression of a search for new lifestyles, new identities, and a desire to show off status. Consumption of big brands gives individuals a sense of cultural identity and distinction from other Chinese people. Many of these young consumers feel that by buying such high-end products, they are more educated, sophisticated, and up to speed with other Western countries.

---

[1] All interviews in this chapter were conducted by the first author, 2008.

Individuals in the upper income bracket live in a similar manner, but with a little more luxury. They showcase their social identity by living in upscale quarters or villas, shuttling around in limousines, frequenting high-class eating establishments, and parading their golf club memberships. Extravagant living is their mantra and business networks only enhance their consumption patterns.

Ken, an MBA-qualified entrepreneur in an engineering company, says:

> I bought my BMW from Hong Kong because China wouldn't have such an import [foreign] car. I wear a Rolex and have the latest models of mobile phones. It isn't because I have to have these luxury items, but it's to show off in front of my buddies and business partners. You drive a luxury car and live in a luxury apartment to represent that you're rich. This is the most important part of attracting someone who you'd like to continue to do business with. With precious and luxury accessories like BMWs, Rolexes and villas or detached houses or even high-storied apartments, I'm in a better position to attract more new business partners (Ken, 30, Entrepreneur).

Alex agrees with Ken. Alex is a graduate from a renowned university and only makes about RMB10,000 a month (US$1,290 or £645). Still, he drives a Chinese-made Honda he bought for RMB350,000 (US$51,210 or £25,605), usually wears the most fashionable and trendy clothes and visits Hong Kong twice a month to buy brand-name products. He says,

> My mottos are 'spend money for tomorrow' or 'realize the dream for today.' No need to worry about tomorrow but seize happiness wholeheartedly in nightclubs with my friends. I don't have 'saving' in my dictionary. Temptations are terribly many in Guangdong. You can find much entertainment and play here. Money runs, money comes, no need to worry too much (Alex, 26, Professional).

Through interviews with Alex we learned that he often travels to Europe and buys famous products. He shared that his monthly salary is not enough to support such a lifestyle, but he does subcontracting trade with entrepreneurs and cadres. Although Alex is married he does not want any children yet. He appears to be worry free and has no financial stress. Alex's story is typical of the young new middle class.

The new middle class in China is becoming more strategic. They are not simply buying products and services because they like them. It has an additional purpose of advancing their careers and building strong business networks or *guanxi*. In doing so, individuals can gain more business contacts. Mary, a French/German-educated accountant explains her story as follows:

> Dress code shows the status and my peer group could spend a whole month's salary to buy brand-named bags like LV, Gucci or others. If we buy counterfeits, we're no different from the blue-collar workers. It's shameful in front of my friends because they can identify whether or not they're fakes. To play safe, I'll buy in Hong Kong or in France. A LV bag is a must-buy item among my peers.

Ada, an entrepreneur in a large garment factory, echoes Mary's attitude:

> I don't have any confidence in the brand-named goods in China since there are so many counterfeits. I'll order the latest LV bag from Paris and ask for shipping. Otherwise, when you wear the latest style of LV bags, [people could see] it's a counterfeit and it'll be awkward and awful. Our business partners measure our wealth and businesses by brand-name products, luxury cars, and apartments [that we have]. Our business partners also calculate and quantify our wealth through what we wear and where we live (Ada, 32, Entrepreneur).

Chiu agrees with Ada and adds that consumption serves an intrinsic function in doing business. He says,

> I prefer buying a car to buying a villa since we can show off our car to our clients. We cannot show off our house directly to them. In face to face meetings, my clients quantify my wealth in terms of my possession of car (whether it is BMWs), watch (whether it is Rolex), and club membership (Ada, 34, Entrepreneur).

Tong adds:

> I prefer buying iPhone or Samsung phone, car or brand-name suit [Prada] since I can show off when I meet my clients. Although I am not a boss, but I need to be more presentable and dress decently when I meet my clients in order to earn bonus and commission from my job (Tong, 35, Professional).

Most of the young generation feels that they can be different from lower class manual workers by wearing a different style of clothing. Some go even as far as eating less food so that they have more money to spend on brand-name items. Ivy, a 26-year-old professional says:

> I think if entrepreneurs want to invest businesses in China, they need to bring some exotic branded goods to Guangdong. They need to show us the certificate of each branded goods with a product code. This can guarantee I won't buy any counterfeit goods. I would feel disgusted if I spent huge amounts of money on buying fake goods (Ivy, 26, Professional).

From these interviews, there is one common trend. The young generation of China's new middle class is not buying high-end products because they need them, but rather their desire to have them (see Photo 2). Certainly the fashion sector is no exception. In

Photo 2: In Guangdong, you can find brand-name stores everywhere. Prada is just one example.

the case of China, fashion functions as a catalyst for uniting yet, excluding individuals of different social classes. For example, politicians and intellectuals are higher on the social pyramid, whereas manual laborers and lower income individuals are on the bottom. This hierarchy creates both exclusion and inclusion of individuals, especially what type of clothes one wears.

When individuals were asked what they would do if they had money, the majority of respondents said they would buy things, clothing in particular. Alex tells us:

> I like to buy fashion from Japan, such as Aape, Porter, Agnes b, Birkenstock and other brand-named products. In fact, we aren't out of fashion but I know we're always giving foreigners the feeling that we're unfashionable. Now, we're quite trendy and much more fashionable than many of the middle class all over the world, including the Hong Kong middle class (Alex, 32, Professional).

Fai agrees with Alex:

I definitely won't buy any local fashion brands and only buy international brands like LV, Gucci, Prada, Jack Jones, Calvin Kelvin, Polo and Burberry. We are not old fashioned at all. There are many large-scale shopping malls in China. How can I avoid the attractions and temptations? (Fai, 28, Professional).

I have different cars. I own a BMW, Ferrari, and Mercedes-Benz which represent my attitude and reflect my quality of life. You don't need the government to tell you to consume, you will smell this in the CCP's policies. Consumerism will definitely strengthen state authority. We are the middle class, I think the only function for us is to pay tax and consume, and buy brand names. This is the safest way to be politically neutral. Who wants to betray the CCP? If you do so, you will disconnect all your business outlets and wayout with the Chinese government. Who will be so foolish to do so? (Tom, early 30, Professional).

Consumption is a major part of the globalization process in China and a primary way to navigate the social system within China. Clearly, a person's fashion sense mirrors his or her middle class social class and status. One possible reason for this might be to dispel the image of being poverty stricken and from the countryside. Thus, by wearing designer clothing the new Chinese middle class can exclude itself from other lower social classes.

The Older Generation of the Chinese New Middle Class

Simply because the young generation of new middle class in China are such consumption experts, do not be fooled by the older generation. One such example is a 40-year-old man whom we will call Uncle Wong. Uncle Wong is a party cadre in Guangdong. He frequently visits Hong Kong and is known for his generosity and lavish spending. During one of his trips, he bought a large amount of valuable jewelry such as jade, gold, diamond-studded watches, and the like. This expenditure alone totaled almost RMB20,000 (US$2,928 or £1,464). Furthermore, he could afford to buy everything using cash.

Uncle Wong's behavior is not unusual amongst China's wealthy. Moreover, success stories such as his were only able to come about thanks to the introduction of market reforms in the late 1970s. This happened when the Chinese government moved to more market-based economy instead of the older state-run model. Moreover, with a more open marketplace, many of the middle class in China can consume not only clothing, but they also seek to improve their living quarters. Many of the middle class live in large homes, about 150 square meters (1,500 square feet). Most have spacious gardens and extra parking which overlook seafronts or hillsides. This is done in an attempt to bring peace and harmony into one's life and mimic a Western lifestyle.

Not only is the outside extravagant, but the inside of many homes are filled with lavish décor that can be worth up to RMB1 million (US$146,316 or £73,158). I had the opportunity to visit such a "dream" home once. It was outfitted with many of the modern conveniences of a highly stylish home and reflected the family's social class. Tsang owns such a dream home[2]:

> I live in a hundred and fifty square meters [home] with my wife and two daughters. I spent about 1 million yuan (US$146,316 or £73,158) to furnish the house. The house isn't just for living, but to live in with taste where my family and I [can] pursue a high quality of life. I didn't just have it designed for luxury but, rather, for a taste for the modern. I bought materials especially from France, Italy, and other European countries to decorate my house. I simply pursued my tastes in living and don't like to follow popular furnishings in China, which I regard as tasteless and without character. We wanted to have our own swimming pool and [now]

---

[2] The interviews were conducted by the author in summer, 2008.

only the residents have the privilege of gaining access [to it] [Tsang, 40, Entrepreneur]

Professionals Raymond and Peter seem to agree with Tsang as does Steve.

Quality of life is very important for me. I don't want a shelter. I demand the art of living. A clubhouse is a must item for me ... [Raymond, 50, Entrepreneur]

... When I invite my business partners to my home, they will see where you live and which brand of car you drive. All relate to business opportunities ... [Peter, 52, Entrepreneur].

Consumption is a social palliative. When compared to the Cultural Revolution, China is on its own way to make progress. I love consumption and politically free. I am 'old bird' (*laojianghu* 老江湖), I knew the Chinese government very well. China won't have the guts to tolerate a second Cultural Revolution or June fourth Incident. We can tell consumption is the right thing for us to do. Actually as a middle class, I don't think we can act like the Western countries. What else can we do except consume and pay taxes? (Steve, mid 30, Professional).

Through the aforementioned first-hand accounts of China's older generation middle class, it is clear that their spending habits are, in some respects equal to those of the young generation. The second generation of the Chinese new middle class are more anxious and uncertain about their future in post-reform China.

Anxiety, Uncertainty, and Individualization between Generations

Although the older generation might have more of an interest in luxury homes and their living conditions than the young generation, they still share the common desire to impress business clients, to elevate their personal careers and maintain social status. But with this self-serving mentality, it appears that the new middle class in China, especially the young generation, has not had to struggle through difficult times their seniors. Most of the older generation experienced the upheavals, stress, and uncertainty of the Great Leap Forward, Cultural Revolution, Economic Reforms since the late 1970s, and even the globalization era. Thus, the older generation of China's middle class developed a more pragmatic lifestyle, especially to cope with change and uncertainty. Such an utilitarian mindset seems to be juxtaposed with the seemingly frivolous spending habits of the young generation.

Looking forward, both the older and young generation of the new middle class will experience concern and uncertainty for transferring their social status and its accompanying benefits to future generations.

The Future of the Chinese New Middle Class

As China's new middle class expands and post-reform China gets more institutionalized, there will also be more changes with regard to what cultural and social capital will be accepted. Culturally, education level will be a key factor in one's entrance into the middle class as well as social networks *guanxi* inherited from their parents. It becomes problematic since the times are changing in China and the globalization era reigns. Will the experiences of the older generation be enough to continue the *guanxi* system? Or will a new model become necessary to move forward with less uncertainty? Only time will tell what track the young generation uses to pursue its future trajectory.

The seemingly antiquated networks that the parents of the new generation needed might not be relevant for their children's generation. The new China offers a feast of networks and experiences to its middle class including study abroad experiences. Not only cultural capital, but also social capital will be necessary for China's expected growing middle class from 600–800 million (Tsang, 2014) in the coming 10.5 years. The young generation brings with it a fresh perspective. Perhaps the young generation's next challenge will be forging its own hybrid *guanxi* networks with global sensitivity.

References

Amaldoss, W., & Jain, S. (2005). Conspicuous Consumption and Sophisticated Thinking. *Management Science, 51*(10): 1449–1466.

Bian, Y. (2001). Guanxi Capital and Social Eating: Theoretical Models and Empirical Analyses. In Lin, N., Cook, K., & Burt, R. (eds.), *Social Capital: Theory and Research.* New York: Aldine de Gruyter, pp. 275–295.

China NBS — National Data (2015) www.data.stats.govcn/english. Retrieved on 29 June 2015.

Gerth, K. (2011). Lifestyles of the Rich and Infamous: Creation and Implications of China's New Aristocracy. *Comparative Sociology, 10*: 488–507.

Goodman, S.G. (2014). Middle Class China: Dreams and Aspirations. *Journal of Chinese Political Sciences, 19*: 49–67.

Guo, C., & Miller, J.K. (2010). Guanxi Dynamics and Entrepreneurial Firm Creation and Development in China. *Management & Organization Review, 6*(2): 267–291.

Guo, Y. (2012). Classes without Class Consciousness and Class Consciousness without Classes: The Meaning of Class in the People's Republic of China. *Journal of Contemporary China, 21*(77): 723–739.

Ma, W., & Cheng, J.Y.S. 2010. The Evolution of Entrepreneurs' Social Networks in China: Patterns and Significance. *Journal of Contemporary China, 19*(67): 891–911.

Podoshen, J.S., Li, L., & Zhang, J. (2011). Materialism and Conspicuous Consumption in China: A Cross-Cultural Examination. *International Journal of Consumer Studies, 35*(1): 17–25.

Portes, A. (1998). Social Capital: Its Origins and Applications in Modern Sociology. *Annual Review of Sociology, 24*: 1–24.

Trigg, A. (2001). Veblen, Bourdieu, and Conspicuous Consumption. *Journal of Economic Issues, 35*(1): 99–115.

Veblen, T. (1899/1934). *The Theory of the Leisure Class: An Economic Study in the Evolution of Institutions.* New York: Macmillan.

Veblen, T. (1924). *The Theory of the Leisure Class: An Economic Study of Institutions.* London: Allen & Unwin.

Chapter 6

Spending without Speaking: China's Middle Class, Governmentality, and Conspicuous Consumption

The previous chapter explored the emergence of the Chinese new middle class and their conspicuous spending habits. This chapter elaborates upon this a bit further by explaining why the Chinese new middle class engage in such activity. This chapter also contends that the shared behavior amongst the middle class is a desire by individuals to flaunt their status, but is also a logical tactic of the Communist Chinese government. The basis for this is Foucault's concept of "governmentality", which states that the government is using the face of consumerism as a means to control and direct the large social force of the middle class. It is grounded in a socialist framework that the Chinese Party-state can control many people, while focusing on the individual. Thus, the middle class feels anxious to conform to the government's interests. This is to distract the public away from thoughts of being involved in political matters.

The ability of the central government to divert the public's attention away from certain matters has taken time, but in recent years the consumer revolution has spread rapidly throughout China. This has resulted in conspicuous consumption, a phenomenon developed by Veblen (1899/1934, Veblen 1924) in the late 19th century. Because of China's low gross domestic product (GDP) per capita, which is in the lower middle-income bracket of countries like Turkmenistan and the Maldives, it seems peculiar that such spending could occur. Moreover, less explored is the relationship between Chinese consumers and the Communist Chinese Party (CCP). To address these question ethnographics were conducted and guided by three particular research questions. (1) Why do the Chinese middle class participate in conspicuous consumption? (2) To what extent can observable conspicuous consumption be accounted for by Veblen's theory? (3) What is the CCP state's role in the emergence of conspicuous consumption? Some derivative questions include is this part of an implicit Chinese governing process and strategy? If so, what are the systemic governmental practices and techniques within which the CCP operates? What does this teach us about the bio-political relationship between the new middle class and the CCP?

The chapter is presented in five sections. It starts from a brief overview of the existing theories of conspicuous consumption and the Foucauldian notion of governmentality. The second section will introduce the target of this research: the post-1970 middle class, followed by a discussion of its conspicuous consumption behavior, as well as the shortcomings of the prevailing theories of conspicuous consumption in explaining the growth of that consumption in reform China. The fifth section will explain the rise of conspicuous consumption in today's China by re-engaging governmentality. The significance of this study and the implications of authoritarian governmentality, will be presented in the conclusion.

Classical Theories on Consumer Culture

Consumption has been studied by students of marketing and sociology. Whereas students of marketing are interested in what affects consumers' choices of goods (see, e.g. Amaldoss & Jain, 2005; Podoshen *et al.*, 2011), sociologists are concerned with social standing and distinctions expressed through consumption. They argue that goods & services bought by the nouveaux rich are purchased with the intention of showing often their social status to others. Therefore, consumption is a marker of social class. Consumer goods are symbols of status, which, in turn, determines consumers' differential access to scarce and valued resources. To put it differently, consumption produces and reproduces social inequality.

Seen from this perspective, consumer culture, defined as the "differentiated" and "market differentiated" culture of modern societies, in which individual tastes not only reflect the social locations (age, gender, occupation, ethnicity, etc.), but also the social values and individual life styles of consumers (Jary & Jary, 1991: 116): consumer culture is a lens through which we can understand the ongoing social change of a globalizing China. Consumer culture and conspicuous consumption are key indicators for class analysis. As consumption becomes a significant source of differentiation of social status and prestige, the ability to assimilate themselves into a "tasteful"consumer culture becomes a tool and survival kit for the Chinese middle class to extend *guanxi* networks and improve their upward social mobility. The growing importance of materialism and consumerism has led to questions about the nature of what are referred to as worldly possessions. In a consumer-driven world, material possessions are seen as the key to happiness, as people's social status is judged by personal success as well as possession of material wealth (Osburg, 2013). Perceptions about self and others are affected by those judgments. Indeed, materialism and happiness-seeking through consumption is a key social norm in Western civilization (Belk, 1985; Campbell, 1987; McCracken, 1988).

Veblen's *The Theory of the Leisure Class* (1899/1934) was the first work that provided insight into the relationship between consumption and class which was discussed in Chapter 5. Not explicitly focusing on conspicuous consumption but all types of consumption notwithstanding, Bourdieu (1984), however, points out that classes are distinguished by cultural differences, especially those in lifestyles. Culture and lifestyle have a direct bearing on social stratification. Social distinction is shaped by, among others, cultural capital, which may take the forms of educational qualifications, artistic appreciation, lifestyles and consumption patterns, and body make-up. People with different lifestyles develop their own *habitus* and people of the same class tend to fit in with each other readily well and form networks of social connections (i.e. "social capital" in Bourdieu's terminology). Bourdieu & Wacquant (1992) emphasize the leading function of education in predisposing an individual or group to engage in certain cultural practices. The inference is that education brings about differential cultural patterns. Class struggles are over what constitute high/elite culture and the defense of high cultural capital by maintaining privileged access to higher education and high cultural objects or practices. A dominant economic class able to gain access to superior culture (e.g. good taste) legitimizes its position of super-ordination relative to other classes. In this paper, Bourdieu's concepts of lifestyles, consumption, taste, *habitus*, and distinction are reconceptualized to account for the emergence of the conspicuous consumption among the young generation. As a deeply ideological category, taste functions as an indicator of class, a group of people who share the same consumer culture and pursue the pleasure of consumption (Bourdieu, 1977, 1984, 1989, 1996, 1999). While Veblen's conspicuous consumption is a form of modernity involving the pursuit of higher class status, Bourdieu's sociology of consumption is a signification and construction of the self. His concept of class *habitus* indicates that cultural capital is the pivotal determinant of values, instincts, and lifestyles.

Consumption of material and cultural goods serves as a primary way in which the Chinese middle class become connected with, and thus integrated into, the social structure (Chen & Goodman, 2013).

Through conspicuous consumption, the middle class have a high sense of cultural superiority with their privileged class position, which differentiates them from other social groups by the consumption of branded and luxury goods and decent housing like gated communities (Pou, 2009; Tang, 2013). In addition, Fung (2010) asserts that conspicuous consumption provides a shelter for rapport and comfort from the emotional and relational problems of real life. Conspicuous consumption, as a social practice and activity, can be a realm of symbolic struggle and change, and is also part of the materialistic culture of Hong Kong, China, and Taiwan. Conspicuous consumption is not only about tangible consumer goods, but also the ideology, status, and culture embedded within shopping and consumption (Fung, 2010: 325). Perceived as a cultural process, consumption and the accompanying identity formation are by definition in what the world is made to appear in a society. This world reflects the interests of certain dominant or powerful classes and groups there (Grossberg, 1984).

These cultural perspectives, however, fail to address why the Chinese Party-state has done little beyond propagandizing to impose control over conspicuous consumption: Why does China not consider imposing a progressive consumption tax to curtail conspicuous consumption, as suggested by Frank (1999) in his study of the American society? Instead the recent Chinese policy of appreciating the value of the *renminbi* against the US dollar indirectly encourages conspicuous consumption, as the imported luxury goods are now less expensive than they were. So why does China tolerate conspicuous consumption but crack down on such social ills such as pornography and political speech on the Internet and social media? The concept of governmentality, proposed by Foucault (1982), provides us a nuanced explanation that links the Chinese government rationality with middle-class consumer behavior. The CCP and the middle class share common interests in working together to achieve a "harmonious society" (*hexie shehui* 和谐社会) as well as a moderately prosperous society (*xiaokang shehui* 小康社会).

Foucauldian Governmentality

With the characteristics of depoliticization at work in a significant number of the Chinese new middle class, the concept of governmentality, coined by Michel Foucault, is relevant to discern the ideologies between the People Republic China/Chinese (PRC) state and the Chinese new middle class. The key to the concept of "governmentality" is that the modern state exercises power from within the individual, while preserving the illusion of freedom, and control is exercised within the individual by the individual. Based on Foucault's (1982: 220–221) definition of government as the "conduct of conduct", governmentality can be defined as "the regulation of conduct using various technical means and [by] encouraging individuals to regulate themselves" (Joseph, 2003: 181). In essence it encompasses all the ways of thinking about how, and the assemblages of tools by which, a population's conduct is governed. The multiple organized practices that the state uses to regulate and shape, by calculated means from a distance, how its population should behave to fulfill the state's policies include not only state institutions but also discourses, norms, and self-regulation (Ferguson & Gupta, 2002).

Governmentality is based upon a "pastoral" approach which can be understood in two contrasting ways. First, the government sets the conditions under which individuals conceived as free citizens regulate their own behavior by following their perceived self-interests and, in doing so, serve the interests of the state (Pierson, 2011: 78–79). Second, it refers to a so-called "shepherd-flock" relation whereby the rulers show concern for the welfare of their populations, stressing the need for social solidarity (Dean, 2010: 90–101).

Existing governmentality studies are, however, often focused on the neoliberal form of governance, a particular mentality of government, whereby the population is governed through their free choices, encouraged by the means of liberal market forces (Joseph, 2012: 25). However, neoliberal governmentality is not about freedom from regulation; rather, it is a very specific form of regulation that emphasizes "rationalised and responsible self-conduct" by responsible individuals, aided by governmental interventions that introduce and extend the norms and values of the market such as enterprise, competition, and risk-taking (Joseph, 2012: 28; Miller & Rose, 2008). This neoliberal form of governance is essentially about self-regulation, "empowerment" or the "responsibilisation" of subjects, enabling them to take individual responsibility for their well-being instead of relying on the welfare state (Lemke, 2001).

In addition, governmentality is concerned with the ways in which the state exercises power over the people by shaping the choices, desires, and lifestyles of individuals and groups, rather than by imposing prohibitions or controls, known as disciplinary power (Dean, 2010: 20). At the core of the governmentality proposed by Foucault is the biopower. The nexus between government and power is that the government tries to reduce the operation of political power to the actions of state, understood as a relatively coherent and calculating political subject. Rather than defining political rule in terms of a state that extends its sway throughout society by means of an apparatus of control, the concept of govermentality draws attention to the diversity of forces and knowledge involved in efforts to regulate the lives of individuals, and the conditions within particular national territories, in pursuit of various goals (Jeffreys, 2009). The power is progressively elaborate, rationalized, and centralized, in the form of, and under the auspices of, state institutions (Foucault, 1982: 208–226). Here, we focus on the neutral meaning of governmentality: the processes or devices the state uses to regulate or shape, from a distance, how people (should) behave within its territory to act in the interests of the state.

There are indications that the CCP is introducing Chinese socialist governmentality. For example, the CCP Central Committee General Office warned party cadres in April 2013 against seven subversive currents prevalent in Chinese society. The "seven perils" are Western constitutional democracy, universal values of human rights, civil-society movement, neo-liberal market economy, press freedom and media independence, nihilist criticism of the Party's history, and criticism of the reform and opening-up policy (Buckley, 2013; Lubman, 2013). Why does the CCP not regard the lavish consumption of luxury goods from the capitalist West — except that by, *but not for*, its cadres — as an imminent threat to China's socialist system? Allowing the seemingly spontaneous development of a profligate consumer culture may be part of the CCP strategy of governmentality that is intended to shape the desires, aspirations and lifestyle of the burgeoning middle class. The idea here is that state bodies, populations, societies, communities, and individuals are driven to "self-regulate" through discourses of security/threat (Foster, 2008). If members of the Chinese middle class are fearful of their security, they will self-censor and modify their own behavior with minimal state government interference. Working in conjunction with the risk-versus-security drive behind governmentality is a discursive link that is "forged between economic prosperity and well-being" (Lemke, 2001: 202).

For the Chinese new middle class, there is clearly a reward system for self-control. The message conveyed to the middle class by the PRC is "if you govern yourself effectively, you will improve your own well-being" (Kerr *et al.*, 2011: 202). More importantly, it may serve the political purpose of preserving the predominant position of the ruling Communist party by both promoting consumption-driven economic growth and diverting the attention of the rising class away from politically divisive and sensitive social issues. For the purpose of this chapter, governmentality is understood as consisting of a three-tiered structure, incorporating self-government (i.e. by the Chinese new middle class), government by the state (i.e. the PRC) and government by others (i.e. by the mass media) (Rutherford, 1999: 46). The Chinese Party-state conveys a message through mass media reports and programs that a proper social attitude should be saying "NO to politics and YES to consumption; I consume, therefore I am." Most of the Chinese middle class remain closely connected to the CCP, refusing to risk losing the benefits obtained from state policies.

In examining whether consumerism is used to support the governance of the CCP, this study supplements and strengthens the growing literature on the application of governmentality to the analysis of contemporary Chinese society as well as consumer behavior (Jeffreys, 2009; Beckett, 2012). Through the lens of governmentality, Beckett (2012) provides an example of how producers construct the identities of consumers (as savvy consumers), and encourage them to identify with the constructed identities, and to reproduce the identities by exercising their freedom to consume. He uses the Clubcard, a loyalty card issued by Tesco, the British largest retailer, as a case study to examine how Tesco employs the Clubcard, perceived as a technology of consumption, to govern the consumption patterns of its consumers.

Target of Investigation: The Young Generation of the Chinese New Middle Class

The participants in this study were 50 young generation adults from Guangdong province and seven cities including Dongguan, Foshan, Guangzhou, Shenzhen, Zhongshan, Zhuhai, and Yangjiang. Their professions ranged from cadres (10), professionals (26), and entrepreneurs (14). There were 28 men and 22 women. All the men and only 10 women were married. Each of the interviewees held bachelors, masters, or even doctorate degrees. They were found by the snowball collection method. I first used my own contacts and then branched out to other friend networks.

The author collected data over three years spanning from 2007 to 2010. Many of those interviewed were born during or after China's Cultural Revolution from 1966 till 1976. This was the benchmark for inclusion in this study. Obviously, those who did live through this event are referred to as the old generation (Tsang, 2013). A significant distinction between these two generations is the degree of materialism that abounds. Prior to this period in China's history, there was more emphasis on political propaganda. Hanser (2008) notes that this generation uses their consumption habits as a symbol of their high social class.

Because Chinese sociologists have not yet developed a concrete definition for the middle class, many use classifying terms such as: income, occupation, education, and consumption (Li, 2010a; Li, 2010b; Lu, 2012; Goodman, 2008; Pow, 2009; Zhou, 2005, 2008). Even in the West, the middle class is unclearly defined and in the simplest form, individuals who do non-manual labor, such as managerial or professional work, own property, and have cultural assets (Savage *et al.*, 1992; Osburg, 2013). Chen & Goodman (2013) expand this definition to include lifestyle and consumption habits define the middle class. Private housing, education healthcare services also describe the new Chinese middle class.

Bourdieu (1984) elaborates further on additional elements that constitute the middle class including various types of economic, cultural and political/social capital. It is important to understand these elements because they are the foundation for how members of the middle class are able to maintain such a lifestyle. Most of the middle class in the sample benefited from the Maoist socialist institutions of urban *danwei* (work units), urban *hukou* (household registration), and *guanxi* (inter-personal networks). Thus, many individuals were private businesspeople, government cadres, state-owned enterprise managers, and other professionals (Li & McElveen, 2013). This criterion helped them be valuable participants in this study.

The interviews were a combination of formal and informal methods which eased communication between participants and researcher. The author used participant and non-participation observations to better understand the lives of the young generation's middle class in China. All of the names use pseudonyms to protect the participants. The author used open-ended questions, which focused on their consumption patterns, their motivations to extend *guanxi* and status in their consumption behavior, the way in which they see their own identity as a member of China's young generation middle class, their negotiation between traditional Chinese norms and Western orientations, and finally their beliefs about government screening of media so it conforms with Chinese cultural values.

From France to China: Bourdieu and the Chinese New Middle Class

The first research question is about why the young generation practice conspicuous consumption. In order to understand the reasons why the middle class behaves the way it does, we must first learn their patterns of consumption. The middle class respondents from Guangdong province had strong preferences regarding consumption of the finest commodities in categories such as fashion, food, housing, cars, and mobile phones. Not surprising, Masidlover & Burkitt (2013) find that the Chinese have changed the shopping landscapes in Europe to accommodate the large demand for wealthy brands such as Prada and LV. This phenomenon was confirmed in the interviews with 45 out of 50 responding that, if they had money, they would buy whatever they wanted.

The Chinese middle class is not only concerned with clothing and fashion, but also land ownership. Most of the Chinese new middle class owns property across China. Their tastes and consumer habits symbolically convey a special status separate from others (Bourdieu, 1984, Bourdieu & Passeron, 1979; Chen & Goodman, 2013). This display of status is shown on the inside of such houses as well in the décor. One such home is owned by Tsang, a 37-year-old, entrepreneur. His home is not only luxurious, but it is built with imported European materials and is a token of the new China.

Consumption of material and cultural goods is the outlet that the middle class uses to get plugged into the social structure of today's China (Chen & Goodman, 2013). Such spending habits make individuals feel that they are exclusive. Ada is age 32 and an entrepreneur in a large garment factory, she echoes Mary's attitude:

> I order the latest LV bag from Paris and ask for shipping. Otherwise, when you carry a supposedly LV bag, [people could see] it's a counterfeit and it'll be awkward and awful. Our business partners measure our wealth and businesses by brand-name products, luxury cars, and apartments [that we have]. … (Ada, 32, Entrepreneur).

As stated previously, restaurants and other food venues are prime places to find the middle class relaxing. Dining out at Western-oriented restaurants sends the impression that they are cultured (Watson & Caldwell, 2005). These are wonderful spaces for friends to mingle together or even meet with business partners. Lily, 30, a professional, said a café served as her third office. In this space she felt very connected with the middle class, but even more, she felt powerful and individualized. The Western "do it yourself" mentality is for many, inspiring. Thus, Western restaurants are non-traditional Chinese public areas for middle class individuals to enjoy their individualized autonomy.

The conspicuous consumption addressed by Veblen and Bourdieu was based on status and class. The luxury consumption is a key separator of the middle class and working class in China. But, these two theorists focused solely on the individual and neglected the role of the state and maintaining the *status quo*. Furthermore, many official Chinese Communist leaders look down upon such a wasteful lifestyle, but they have yet to stop such fanatical consumption. This was exemplified when the Chinese government appreciated the renminbi's value against the US dollar. This made it easier than ever before for the Chinese to buy high-end products. Foucault's 1980 notion of governmentality links the *habitus* of the Chinese middle class with the CCP government's goals of bringing the country together in harmony.

Re-Engaging France: Foucault and the Chinese Middle-Class Conspicuous Consumption

In order to answer the second research question, that is, why does the Chinese Party-state not curtail conspicuous consumption? Can the lack of action be perceived as a form of governmentality? Economic progress has led to the rise of a new middle class and thus a new social dynamic. Individuals are reconstructing their identities within various classes more on possessions than on professions (Liechty, 2003). In the previous section, governmentality explained why the middle class and its government work closely together. This section addresses the rise of consumption in China, using the lens of governmentality.

There are two layers to the bond of the middle class consumption practices and governmentality. The first is for those unique consumption patterns which differentiate them between other social classes. The second layer is the practice of giving gifts, because it maintains the flow of relations within the Chinese hierarchical culture. These two cultural elements are the foundation of China's conspicuous consumption.

Consumption can be seen as a smooth river that needs to be continually fed to keep life. Likewise, the Chinese government wants to create reasonable prosperity or *xiaokang* [小康] and a harmonious society or *hexieshehui* [和谐社会] by the end of 2020 (Jeffreys, 2009: 23). To some extent, the Chinese government allows the new middle class to govern itself, in order to improve its own well-being (Kerr *et al.*, 2011: 202). This motivates many to comply with government policies and to maintain social cohesion.

> The state and its agents played a central role dominating the public sphere. City squares, auditoriums, and workers' club became sties of state disciplining and for citizens, spaces where support of the CCP's socialist goals where unquestionable. In order to constantly remind us what proper revolutionary behaviour entailed, socialist slogans and posters supressing revolutionary activities typically

covered public walls, theme park, and some shopping malls with lots of CCP's slogan. These were daily reminders for people to uphold the goas of the socialist society like *xiandaihua* (现代化): achieve the four modernisations, *weirenmin fuwu* (为人民服务): serve the people. I can see it clearly in our community (Joseph, professional, early 40).

Harmonious society praise redress for sure. We are the middle class, the government is afraid the numbers of the middle class is getting stronger. The number of the middle class is expanding. The government needs to buy out the middle class to maintain the stability of the government. If I and other middle class are politically conservative, it will be much easier for the government to enact policies (Ben, Professional, late 30).

I will spend tomorrow's money today. I won't follow my parents' lead in hedging bets by saving for the future. I ushered in the idea of immediate retail gratification. Right now, I have money, I can buy whatever I want. The government actually likes this approach a lot. I am young and professional, the government really wants us to spend our energy on bolstering economy, instead of like Hong Kong's youth to avocate social movement (Professional, early 30)

Many influential regional government cadres shared in the interviews that the government wants them to push the ideas of social harmony, but within limits. The middle class knows they must rely on the central government because they are the ones who give them their paycheck. Thus, cadres collaborate with professionals and businesspeople to expand their businesses. They invest, travel and buy housing from the government but never discuss politics.

Likewise, Chinese professionals expressed a similar situation. Many were not in favor of state authoritarianism. But at present, they feel satisfied with their living conditions and thus maintain sociopolitical stability. Entrepreneurs and cadres are more conservative in nature. They prefer an authoritarian state and abide by its principles.

In addition, the influential regional cadres in this sample mentioned that the Central Government is actively promoting consumerism in China. Many are required to make business deals with overseas companies and startup businesses, even in environmentally unsafe areas. Uncle Fang, aged 49, is an influential local cadre. His work unit often listens to professors from Tsinghua University who lecture about ways the Chinese government can increase economic growth while remaining distant from politics. He says,

The interviews with the Chinese middle class revealed that their roles are to pay taxes and stimulate economic growth in China. They focus on business, investment, and enjoyment. Indeed, these middle class individuals interviewed were only a small sampling of the many thousands of cadre government workers who propagate such mottos. This certainly does not diminish the central government's role. Zhang (1996) notes that the government must balance its display of power and authority while promoting the open market system and free enterprise.

In addition, gift giving is an elaborate version of governmentality at work in the China's new middle class.

> Gift giving becomes an institutionalized policy (*guoce* 國策). Our leaders from our team always encourage gift giving to beef up economic growth. They also remind us of the need to forge collaborations with the so-called influential people in society in order to shift people's attention to economic development without harming political stability. Our leaders are really concerned that the influential people like entrepreneurs and professionals will arouse the public to confront the central and local governments (Fang, 49, cadre).

When gifts are given status is not the only idea being displayed, but it is also an opportunity for relationship development or social capital with state cadres. Consumption is a new form of governmentality. It is grounded in the exploitation of the middle classes' desires while satisfying regulations of the central government.

Mass Media

Another promoter of conspicuous consumption and a form of governmentality is mass media. The Chinese new middle class has access to many independent news sources in both Chinese and English languages, but still little interest is given toward political issues. Much of the middle class is indoctrinated by this consumer culture that financial news stories are typically the most read parts of newspapers. Political issues are rarely discussed in middle class newspapers such as the *Southern Metropolitan Newspapers*, *Zhuhai Daily*, *Guangzhou Daily*, and *China Daily*. Even if the middle class's rights to housing and other shares information are under seige, many rarely defy the government.

In recent years, the middle class has engaged in blogging and use mobile phone apps such as *weibo*, QQ, and WeChat. Wang (2013) notes that Microblog users reached 195 million in 2012. The Internet facilitates more information about Chinese political developments and provides the necessary social basis for communication and interaction. Still, the media continues to be censored. Threatening social movements such as the Falun Gong, uprisings in Xinjiang Uyghur and Tibetan areas are extremely guarded by the government. Not surprisingly, consumption advertisements such as Taobao (淘宝), xiecheng (携程), and other online shopping websites spread the mantra of consumerism. A plethora of information is transmitted via the Internet and mobile devices. Even social networking sites, like renren (人人), weibo (微博), and QQ (a Chinese version of MSN) are places for acquiring information. Many of today's generation find comfort in a world full of digital distractions. This can causes people to become increasingly disconnected about the political world.

Still active roles in government by citizens are forbidden. The issues most often discussed in online environments continue to revolve around consumerism topics such as property investments, traveling, and retirement. Many remain concerned about rising property prices and overcrowding in China. Wang (2013) notes that in 2013, property prices in Beijing peaked at around 20,000 yuan per square meter, a 25% increase from the average price of 16,057 yuan per square meter in 2009 (p. 35). In addition, Chinese outbound investment in real estate has jumped to more than US$8 billion in 2013 from US$2 billion in 2012 and the buying spree has started to extend from gateway cities to secondary ones (Wang, 2013). The whole China focuses on economic spending, but not politics. Wang (2013) demonstrate the example of how governmentality distracts US from politics.

Mass media is crucial to spreading cultural beliefs of consumerism to the Chinese new middle class. Global media corporations are trying to spread Western culture into China as well (Djao, 2002: 365). In China today, it is difficult to know what is truth and what is fiction, especially from the media.

Regardless, mass media in China can be used as a means of controlling its citizens and constitutes a form of governmentality. This social order is structured in three ways with the new Chinese middle class, the PRC government, and the mass media (Rutherford, 1999: 46). A harmonious and open relationship among the three are crucial for China's current success.

Conclusion

This chapter used the lens of governmentality to better understand the consumption interests of China's new middle class. It also explored the role of mass media in shaping the beliefs of its citizenry. Through interviews with government cadres, there is some evidence the Chinese Communist Party is deliberately trying to sidetrack its population from political issues by turning the focus on consumerism. The central government has created an environment where citizens' behaviors are being moderated by an age-old practice of gift giving and desire to maintain *guanxi* or connections in efforts to maintain a stable and harmonious nation.

In studying conspicuous consumption in today's China, this article has shed light first on class divisions in contemporary China. The results will likely spark a revisit of the applicability of conventional class theories to China, which is often regarded as a hybrid capitalist–socialist country. We may need to analyze the Chinese people's class location less on the traditional economic indicators of market position, occupation, or possession of the means of production (i.e. economic capital) but rather on such cultural factors as lifestyle or consumption patterns. Second, this chapter has also engaged the ongoing lively debate about the prospects of democratization in China as a result of the emerging new middle class. While conventional wisdom has it that the middle class is often a crucial agent for political transformation and transparency in many parts of the world, there are indications the CCP is undertaking a social engineering process of controlling its population "from within" by directing their activities towards the pursuit of hedonistic consumption. The implications offer an intrigoing perspective on the study of state-society relations in post-reform China, it may be time to analyze China's social stratification and class formation from a new cultural angle. Second, we should pay attention to the governance capacity of the CCP in the "conduct of conduct" (i.e. shaping, guiding, or affecting the behavior and desires) of the Chinese people. Compared with other autocratic regimes in the developing world, the Chinese Party-state is more resilient in adapting governance to emergent social forces and changes that accompany economic growth. This chapter has demonstrated that Party-state cadres form a core element of the rising middle class in China, confirming the need to extend the prevailing study of governmentality to a non-liberal political setting.

Future research on conspicuous consumption, governmentality, and the middle class may be conducted either comparatively or using a more nuanced approach, such as through the survey method. Therefore, additional research may look at different urban areas of China. Comparing diverse areas from the coastal region to interior China may help enhance the generalizability of the findings.

References

Amaldoss, W., & Jain, S. (2005). Conspicuous Consumption and Sophisticated Thinking. *Management Science, 51*(10): 1449–1466.

Beckett, A. (2012). Governing the Consumer: Technologies of Consumption. *Consumption Markets & Culture, 15*(1): 1–18.

Belk, R.W. (1985). Materialism: Trait Aspects of Living in the Material World. *Journal of Consumer Research, 12*: 265–280.

Bourdieu, P. (1977). *Outline of a Theory of Practice.* Cambridge: Cambridge University Press.

Bourdieu, P. (1984). *Distinction: A Social Critique of the Judgment of Taste.* Cambridge: Harvard University Press.

Bourdieu, P. (1996). *The Rules of Art: Genesis and Structure of the Literary Field (Translation and Introduction).* London: Polity.

Bourdieu, P., & Passeron, J.C. (1979). *The Inheritors: French Students and Their Relation to Culture.* Translated by Nice, R. University of Chicago Press.

Bourdieu, P., & Wacquant, J.D. (1992). *An Invitation to Reflexive Sociology.* Chicago: University of Chicago Press.

Bourdieu, P. *et al.*, (1999). *The Weight of the World: Social Suffering in Contemporary Society.* Cambridge: Polity Press.

Buckley, C. (19 August 2013). China Takes Aim at Western Ideas. *New York Times.* Retrieved on 9 September 2013 from http://www.nytimes.com/2013/08/20/world/asia/chinas-new-leadership-takes-hard-line-in-secret-memo.html.

Campbell, J.Y. (1987). Stock Returns and the Term Structure. *Journal of Financial Economics, 18*(2): 373–399.

Chen, M., & Goodman, D.S.G. (eds.) (2013). *Middle Class China: Identity and Behaviour.* Cheltenham: Edward Elgar.

Dean, M. (2010). *Governmentality Power and Rule in Modern Society.* London. Sage.

Djao, W. (2002). Opinion Status as Ethnic Identity in the Chinese Diaspora. *Journal of Contemporary Asia, 32*(3): 363–380.

Ferguson, J., & Gupta, A. (2002). Spatializing States: Toward an Ethnography of Neoliberal Governmentality. *American Ethnologist, 29*(4): 981–1002.

Foster, E.A. (2008). Sustainable Development Policy in Britain: Shaping Conduct through Global Governmentality. *British Politics, 3*(4): 535–555.

Foucault, M. (1982). The Subject and Power. In Dreyfus, H.L. & Rabinow, P. (eds.), *Michel Foucault: Beyond Structuralism and Hermeneutics*. New York: Harvester Wheatsheaf, pp. 208–226.

Frank, R.H. (1999). *Luxury Fever: Why Money Fails to Satisfy in an Era of Excess*. New York: The Free Press.

Fung, A. (2010). Women's Magazines: Construction of Identities and Cultural Consumption in Hong Kong. *Consumption Markets & Culture*, 5(4): 321–336.

Goodman, S.G. (2008). *The New Rich in China: Future Rulers, Present Lives*. London & New York: Routledge.

Grossberg, L. (1984). Strategies of Marxist Cultural Interpretation. *Critical Studies in MASS communication*, 1(4): 392–421.

Hanser, A. (2008). *Service Encounters: Class, Gender, and the Market for Social Distinction in Urban China*. Stanford: Stanford University Press.

Jary, D., & Jary, J. (1991). *Collins Dictionary of Sociology*. London: HarperCollins.

Jeffreys, E. (2009). Governmentality, Governance and China. In: Jeffrey, E. (ed.), *China's Governmentalities: Governing Change, Changing Government*. Abingdon: Routledge.

Joseph, J. (2003). *Social Theory: Conflict, Cohesion and Consent*. Edinburgh: Edinburgh University Press.

Joseph, J. (2012). *The Social in the Global: Social Theory, Governmentality and Global Politics*. Cambridge: Cambridge University Press.

Kerr, P., Byrne, C., & Foster, E. (2011). Theorising Cameronism. *Political Studies Review*, 92(2): 193–207.

Lemke, T. (2001). Paper Presented at the Rethinking Marxism conference, University of Amherst (MA), September 21–24, 2000.

Li, C. (Ed.) (2010a). *China's Emerging Middle Class: Beyond Economic Transformation*. Washington, DC: Brookings Institution Press.

Li, C.L. (2010b). Characterizing China's Middle Class: Heterogeneous Composition and Multiple Identities. In Li, C. (ed.), *China's Emerging Middle Class: Beyond Economic Transformation*. Washington, DC: Brookings Institution Press, pp. 135–156.

Li, C., & McElveen, R. (2013). Can Xi Jinping's Governing Strategy Succeed? www.brooking.edu. Retrieved on 13 June 2014.

Liechty, M. (2003). *Suitably Modern: Making Middle Class Culture in a New Consumer Society*. Princeton: Princeton University Press.

Lu, X. (ed.), (2012). *Social Structure of Contemporary China*. Singapore: World Scientific Publishing.

Lubman, S. (27 August 2013). Document No. 9: The Party Attacks Western Democratic Ideals. *Wall Street Journal*. Retrieved on 9 September 2013 from http://blogs.wsj.com/chinarealtime/2013/08/27/document-no-9-the-party-attacks-western-democratic-ideals/.

Masidlover, N., & Burkitt, L. (2013). In Paris, Chinese Shopping-Tour Buses Go Out Of Fashion. *Wall Street Journal*. Retrieved on 27 July 2013 from http://online.wsj.com/article/SB10001424127887323664204578609452047467788.html.

McCracken, G.D. (1988). *Culture and Consumption*. Bloomington: Indiana University Press.

Miller, P., & Rose, N. (2008). *Governing the Present*: *Administering Economic, Social and Personal Life*. Cambridge: Polity Press.

Osburg, J. (2013). *Anxious Wealth*: *Money and Morality among China's New Rich*. Stanford: Stanford University Press.

Pierson. C. (2011). *The Modern State*. Abingdon: Routledge.

Podoshen, J.S., Lu, L., & Zhang, J.F. (2011). Materialism and Conspicuous Consumption in China: A Cross-Cultural Examination. *International Journal of Consumer Studies*, *35*(1): 17–25.

Pow, C.-P. (2009). *Gated Communities in China*: *Class, Privilege and the Moral Politics of the Good Life*. Abingdon: Routledge.

Rutherford, P. (1999). The Entry of Life into History. In Darier, E. (ed.), *Discourses of the Environment*. Oxford: Blackwell, pp. 37–62.

Savage, M. *et al.* (1992). *Property, Bureaucracy and Culture*: *Middle-Class Formation in Contemporary Britain*. London: Routledge.

Tang, B. (2013). Urban Housing-Status-Groups: Consumption, Lifestyles and Identity. In Chen, M., &. Goodman, D.S.G. (eds.), Middle Class China Identity and Behaviour. MA: Edward Elgar Publishing Inc, pp. 54–74.

Tsang, E.Y.H. (2013). The Quest for Higher Education by the Chinese Middle Class: Retrenching Social Mobility? *Higher Education*, *66*(6): 653–668.

Veblen, T. (1899/1934). *The Theory of the Leisure Class*: *An Economic Study in the Evolution of Institutions*. New York: Macmillan.

Veblen, T. (1924). *The Theory of the Leisure Class*: *An Economic Study of Institutions*. London: Allen & Unwin.

Wang, X. (2013). Desperately Seeking Status: Political, Social and Cultural Attributes of China's rising middle class. *Modern China Studies*, *20*(1): 1–44.

Watson, J.L., & Caldwell, M.L. (2005). *The Cultural Politics of Food and Eating: A Reader*. London: Blackwell Publishing.

Zhang, K. (1996). Jianli Shehuizhuyi Shichang Jingji Xuyao Qianghua Zhengfu Zhineng. It is a need to strengthen the government role under the socialist economy.

Part III
Socio-Cultural Changes
in the Chinese Societies

Chapter 7

Institutionalization of *Guanxi* (Connections)

Probably many people will be familiar with the old American adage — it is not *what* you know but *whom* you know. In American society it can be as simple as your friend introducing you to another friend and because of his help you land a new job in a high-end technology firm. China also has its own system of networking. It is called *guanxi*. This practice can be crucial to successful commercial activity for both Chinese and foreigners involved in these transactions.

Guanxi are very important in China because there are regulations that need to be met and understood to maximize opportunities. Cadres or local government officials discussed earlier in this book have the task of connecting people and individuals. Many times this can mean the success or failure of a business deal.

Some scholars have referred to this as a "moral attitude" within kinship or a circle of friends and acquaintances. (Faure, 2008: 485). Bian (1994, 2002a, 2002b) puts *guanxi* in the context of the new Chinese middle class. *Guanxi* is the dyadic, particular, and sentimental tie that has the potential to facilitate exchanges of favors between parties connected by the tie. Close relationships (called affective or emotive *guanxi*) contain strong expectations of cooperation. The strongest of such exist in family ties, making the parties "one of the family" or "one of us". For each Chinese citizen it is a lifelong task to develop and maintain *guanxi* networks (Lin, 2001, Zhou & Pei, 1997).

Since 1980, post-reforms have allowed business cadres to meet professionals and expand *guanxi* networks across China. Wank (1995) notes that Chinese government institutionalized policies coupled with informal connections were the main factors advancing business. Today, the Chinese economy has developed faster than the regulatory government institutions. For example, there are many loopholes allow insiders the advantage and much is not regulated. The new middle class and others often exploit these weaknesses in the system for personal or monetary profit. *Guanxi* is one main example of this unclear area of Chinese culture. This allows entrepreneurs to seize opportunities.

In the beginning it can be taxing on both one's time and means to find the right *guanxi*. But, in the long term, it will certainly pay off. Over one's lifetime, these *guanxi* will grow and change but one common and frequent practice include social gatherings.

In China, it is practically expected, to respect, maintain, and improve connections with local cadres by means of gift-giving (Yang, 1989, 1994). This is most important during Chinese Lunar New Year and Mid-Autumn Festival. Gifts are more than delicious moon cakes, but usually accompanied with large amounts of cash (see Photos 1 and 2).

> Gift giving is a cycle that can determine one's wage, business contracts, or donations. Many of the interviewees stressed the importance of these relationships. They frequently referenced the maxim, "The more gifts you provide, the more business opportunities you will get. The more you pay, the more you gain". Spending money is a means of making money.

> There are other forms of *guanxi* that are less tangible than money. Trust is essential. Keeping promises and treating others with respect. Of course there are risks with this system. When something

Photo 1: **Most of the Chinese new middle class practice gift-giving such as luxury Chinese wines.**

Photo 2: **Gift giving is a popular socio-cultural practice for the Chinese new middle class to their clients and customers. It is an example of *guanxi* in practice.**

goes wrong, relationships become strained and friends can quickly disappear. This usually occurs when someone feels they were overcharged and not given a fair price on something.

Business disputes are settled differently than in the US. First, the judicial system is uncertain. China has business contract laws, but enforcing them is completely different. First of all, for example, a judge could rule in ones favor, but the court will not carry out the action. This is mainly because of the political nature of the job and judges want to retain their own good *guanxi* standing as well. Secondly, it is difficult to know exactly which agency should handle the case. The fluid and closed nature of the court system makes these decisions appear arbitrary. Therefore, it is important to have *guanxi* that could help solve the situation on your behalf, such as an. Uncle who can directly and privately get a judge or clerk to help the case be resolved.

Guanxi also serves a more practical purpose. Personal relationships are necessary in the marketplace and all facets of Chinese society. They take time to develop, unlike price negotiations. The spoken, rather than written contract works best when parties equally rely on each other. The word *guanxi* originates from Confucian thought meaning "mutual responsibility". Indeed this word has been modified for the business world.

To Western corporations, the move into China's *guanxi* world could be misunderstood. Payoffs and gift giving to one's boss or supervisor might appear unethical, especially in some Western countries. Furthermore, the Chinese business model emphasizes relationships, whereas the Western model is built around the transaction. It is common for Chinese companies to buy certain products at a higher price not because of the interest of the company alone, but because of the duty of upholding the *guanxi* that it has with other companies. To some degree, it is an employee's obligation to point the company toward a close family friend who buys what your company makes. An American equivalent could be the common practice in large corporations of "wining and dining" in hopes to strike a better business transaction.

Photo 3:   Chinese police confiscate routinely illegal hawkers' wares. Unless you or your friends have a relationship or *guanxi* with the police, it is an issue!

Some Western-oriented companies have developed ways of coping with Chinese *guanxi*. The least popular and problematic strategy is to disrupt the cycle which is viewed as disrespectful, culturally insensitive, and worse yet, loses the business relationship. But many foreign companies prefer embracing *guanxi* in calmer ways. They hire Chinese-born bilingual cadres who are often educated in the West. Even still, this strategy might not always work simply because of the strong cultural affiliation of the Chinese with *guanxi* (see Photo 3).

Navigating *guanxi* is no simple task, even for native Chinese. But in the corporate world there should be a line that can satisfy both cultures. This calls for a blending of Western corporate culture and the *guanxi* culture of China. Once fully understood, the proper balance between favoritism and obligation can be made and be implemented.

I have found that most of the middle-class families are well networked   and   have   ties   with   ex-colleagues   (cadres)   or acquaintances (social capital) in the private university. It will be easy for them to bring their children to it. Although most private universities accept students based on the scores attained in the national entrance examination in China, they still have quotas for self-discretion, giving rise to "memo students" and "connections" students. The memo students are the students whose parents were cadres-turned-entrepreneurs or professionals. Their parents have the backing of *danwei* and have urban *hukou*, and have close connections with their acquaintances who have the same background (*guanxi*) and political capital in Guangdong. Urban *hukou* is still important for the old generation to help their children to study in key primary and secondary schools, and private universities. Fong (Annie's mother) said her urban *hukou* allowed Annie to study in key schools and the private university. The key schools teach English in their formal curriculum and the private university has a mission of advancing the internationalization of Chinese quality education, while at the same time taking the lead in implementing liberal arts education in China (Woronov, 2008). The private university offers a number of unique features. First, it is an international school with unique educational approaches blending elements of Chinese and Western educational models. Second, it provides small-class teaching and numerous extracurricular activities. Third, English is the primary medium of instruction. Fourth, it emphasizes the importance of education, critical or creative thinking, and the balance between formal study and extracurricular activities. Most of the Chinese new middle-class parents who do not want their children to be exposed to political propaganda are also impressed by the flexibility it offers.

Fong was aware that a degree from a second tier, publicly-run university would not help Annie find a good career. Annie earned a high grade point average (GPA) at my previous private university. With a strong desire for Annie to study abroad, Fong collected a lot of information about overseas study and universities. She sought help from ex-colleagues in the government and consultancy agencies in Guangdong while Annie was studying in her first year at the private university. Fong paid RMB100,000 to the agencies which guaranteed that Annie could get a place in one of the top 50 universities in the USA. If she failed to get an offer, the agent would refund the money. In September 2010, Annie was admitted to a prestigious university in the US.

Similar to Annie, Raymond got an offer from New York University in the US in 2010. His mother, Yan, had a back-up plan. Yan has very broad connections with professionals, cadres, and entrepreneurs. If Raymond could find a job in the US, it would be better for him to work in China before her retirement. Yan understood that after retirement, her *guanxi* would no longer pay any dividends. Given that some graduates from Fudan University (the top ranked university in Shanghai) could not even find a job, she was anxious about her son's future. "*Guanxi* is considered significant in future job-seeking. Thus, even if they earned a PhD from a very good university in the US or even China, it is hard for people to get a good job". Raymond echoed his mother's concerns and followed her plan. With his mother's back-up plan, he was at ease. In general, the second-generation middle class prefer working in the US. But if they fail to get work in the US, they still have connections to get a job in China.

The above accounts illustrate that the old generation of the Chinese middle class cultivate their social networks, derived from both *danwei* and *hukou*, to help their children maintain their middle class status. A considerable amount of fortune is often reserved exclusively for their children's future. To prevent any possible demotion along the social strata, the Chinese new middle class resorts to extensive investment in social connections and ways of life, especially regarding their one and only child. Most of the middle-class children show characteristics of a "post-communist personality" (Wang, 2002; Faure, 2008: 476), are well-planned, flexible to change, individualistic, ambitious, and aspirational in their career planning. With losing "face" being a concern deeply ingrained in Chinese culture, they are at pains to find a good career in order not to ruin both their family reputation and their own individual career path.

Meanwhile, some Chinese students already abroad try to earn international work experience (as well as to cope with living expenses). With that kind of overseas work experience, the returnees become much better positioned to get hired back home and more likely to be in the pipeline for promotions than local graduates. In some of my case studies, middle-class parents even intentionally created opportunities for their daughters to have acquaintance with well-off men in the hope that they would get married in the future. All these corroborate the view that the young generation who have been educated overseas, are bound to have better life chances than their counterparts who are locally educated. That, in turn, fuels the need for people to receive overseas education, heightening the need to succeed in the education system at home and abroad.

In addition, *guanxi* is not simple cultural practices in China. A good job placement is often "bought" in cash or in kind. The pulling of connections can be complicated as well — favors are done not through a "friend", but a "friend's friend" or a "colleague's acquaintance" or a "neighbor's relative". The complexities of these connections are important for the old generation to help their children find a job. Lu, a businessman in Guangzhou, has close business dealings with one of the local banks in downtown Guangzhou. He has, in particular, very close connections with the bank director, Paul. However, Paul could not help Lu to find a job for Joel, Lu's son, since only the headquarters in Beijing could make a job offer to Joel. Influenced by Lu's strong *guanxi* ties with him, Paul took the initiative to invite the President in Beijing to have an inexpensive meal to persuade him to offer Joel a job in the bank. Within circles of close *guanxi*, people are more likely to apply *renqing*; Paul values obligation rather than gift-giving and banqueting. They value *ganqing* (*zhong ganqing*) rather than *renqing wei* (showing human kindness). Lu and the president of the bank did not know each other. But they had a common friend, Paul, to bring them together.

Confucian virtues (*renyi*), affection (*ganqing*), obligation, the strong ties of *guanxi* network between Lu and Paul go beyond gift giving and tangible monetary rewards. If Lu were not a close friend of Paul, Joel cannot successfully secure a job in Guangdong, though Lu gave an expensive meal and gifts to Paul.

In the coming decades, economists project China to become the leading economy in the world. *Guanxi* networks were a strong force in the past and most certainly will continue. The ability of Western companies to adapt and use this practice to their advantage can provide them a key competitive advantage.

Conclusion

This article investigated the relative importance of cultural practices of *guanxi* in post-reform China, especially in Guangdong province. While China's new middle class are a privileged group, they still have to fully utilize their *guanxi* network in their everyday lives and practices. They still have to rely on cadres, parental social capital, and trust-generating *guanxi* networks in order to have a chance at a successful career. These elements together play an influential role in affecting intergenerational mobility of the modern Chinese middle class. A socio-cultural perspective, after incorporating the "cultural turn" of Bourdieuian theory on class, argues for the importance of studying the role of social institutions in shaping *habitus* and human agency. It both sheds light on the possibility of social mobility in post-reform China and reveals the enduring importance of cadres, *guanxi* and trust, bound by the historic socialist social institutions of *hukou* and *danwei*, in class (re) production.

Despite the fact that parents in middle-class families may not have advanced education or qualifications (mainly due to the breakdown of the higher education system in the years of political turmoil), they usually have greater currency of social capital, maintained by the networks and ties with their *danwei*, than their children. They have such networks due to the nature of their own occupations and professions. This chapter provided a socio-cultural perspective on how the Chinese new middle class make use of social capital to preserve or enhance intergenerational mobility. These processes help explain how and why socialist social institutions continue to impact the life chances and intergenerational mobility of the new middle class. On the one hand, Chinese "Tier 1" cities such as Shanghai and Beijing in post-reform China are economically advanced and mirror the activities and processes of other equally cosmopolitan global cities; on the other, finding jobs and getting promoted are, however, highly dependent on *guanxi* and state patronage. The Chinese middle class who are employed in state enterprises or private corporations are closely linked with the ruling Communist Party via cadre-centered *guanxi* networks. They are the primary beneficiaries of statism in the wake of current economic reform and globalization. The development of the middle class is heavily dependent upon state power because it is through this mechanism that they make advantage of the existing "old boy" networks to maintain intergenerational mobility. The *guanxi*-based system helps ensure this class can perpetuate itself, hold its middle-class status, enjoy its distinctive materialist lifestyles, and most importantly will not challenge the communist regime. A direct implication of this development is whether social connections with resourced and powerful contacts continue to play a significant role in the labor market. Attention should rather be given to whether social capital has become a crucial means of perpetuating social inequality and social stratification through the generations in reform China. This chapter demonstrates that urban middle-class families go to great lengths to mobilize and use their social capital to advance their children's career. As social division and exclusion in present-day China can no longer be legitimately based on where one is, the vested interested urban groups — the urban middle class in our case — try to preserve their institutionally constructed advantages by transforming the norms about social division and exclusion into one based on what one has, hence the growing importance of cultural and social capitals.

References

Bian, Y.J. (1994). *Work and Inequality in Urban China*. Albany, New York: State University of New York Press.

Faure, G.O. (2008). Chinese Society and Its New Emerging Culture. *Journal of Contemporary China, 17*(56): 469–491.

Lin, N. (2001). Social Capital: A Theory of Structure and Action. Cambridge: Cambridge University Press.

Wang, X. (2002). The Post-Communist Personality: The Spectre of China's Capitalist Market Reforms. *The China Journal, 47*: 1–18.

Wank, D.L. (1995). Bureaucratic Patronage and Private Business: Changing Networks Of Power In Urban China. In Walder, A.G. (ed.), *The Waning of the Communist State: Economic Origins of Political Decline in China and Hungary*. Berkeley: University of California Press, pp. 153–183.

Woronov, T. (2008). Migrant Children and Migrant Schooling: Policies, Problems and Possibilities. In Murphy, R. (ed.), *Labour Migration and Social Development in Contemporary China*. Abingdon, Oxon: Routledge, pp. 96–114.

Yang, M. (1989). Between State and Society: The Construction of Corporateness in a Chinese socialist factory. *Australian Journal of Chinese Affairs, 22*: 31–60.

Yang, M. (1994). *Gifts, Favours and Banquets: The Art to Social Relationships in China*. Ithaca, New York: Cornell University Press.

Zhou, X.G., & Pei, X.M. (1997). Chinese Sociology in a Transitional Society. *Contemporary Sociology, 26*: 569–572.

Chapter 8

Consumerism, the Pursuit of Beauty and Medical Tourism

The time-honored maxim "Beauty is in the eyes of the beholder" is taken literally in the hearts of many of China's women. Euromonitor International's Countries and Consumers (2012) report that working women contribute greatly to the consumption of beauty and personal care products. With higher salaries and prospects for higher education, women today see yesterday's luxury as today's necessity. This chapter explores women's consumerism behaviors in post-reform China. The first section discusses popular services ranging from cosmetic surgery to foreign products. It also describes the role that beauty and looks plays in job success. The next part discusses in greater detail health-related products and industries followed by new-age health movements and their implications for Chinese society.

China is the world's fourth largest beauty and personal care market, just behind the US, Japan, and Brazil (Euromonitor International, 2012). Experts project that by 2015 China's beauty and personal care consumption will reach US$34 billion (£17 billion). A large portion of this will be in skin care products. On a sunny day, it is common to see women in China with umbrellas protecting their skin.

Some Chinese culture observers have noted that the vast majority of Chinese women are extremely insecure about their physical appearance, even more than the West. They know how to dress and they dress in colorful and very feminine clothing. They want to maximize the effect of a good body shape. This causes many women to have a strong sense for fashion. They fancy fashion, adornments, match and mix, and they pay more attention to fashion trends.

Chinese women care a lot about their age as well as their beauty regardless of the fact that often it is said that Chinese women look younger than their actual age. Cosmetic surgery is very popular in China. Other skin treatments and spa treatments are also very popular.

Photo 1: In China people, especially women are increasingly concerned about beauty and health.

Photo 2: **Many Chinese women pay attention to detail and wear fashionable clothes. Increasingly they are choosing Western clothing styles to convey an international image.**

To understand the beauty culture in China and its effect on women, one must first understand that Chinese women experience great social pressure to be extremely thin. Parents, friends, teachers, and commercial advertisements constantly remind women of this. Many ads also feature light-skinned Western models or those of Eurasian ancestry. This has created a stigma associated with dark skinned Chinese women go beyond go their means to buy expensive whitening creams. More wealthy women can afford "corrective" plastic surgery, including hymnography or the surgical restoration of the hymen (see Photos 2 and 3).

Plastic surgery has become common in post-reform China. It has become so popular that in 2004, China hosted its first beauty pageant exclusively for women who had cosmetic procedures (ABC News, 2008). Although these procedures raises safety concern, many

Photo 3:   Appearing extremely feminine is popular in China, a farcry from the days of Unisex Mao jackets.

women are willing to go to great lengths to improve their features. These women go to private or public hospitals to get this kind of surgery. Prices vary from a few thousand RMB (less than US$1,000) to several hundred thousand. Last year there were over 3 million plastic surgery operations in mainland China. Figures released by the government media show aggregate spending for those procedures surpassed US$2 billion. Some women will also go to Hong Kong, South Korea, the US, or even Suzhou, China to have this artificial surgery (ABC News, 2008).

Many women undertake such procedures because they do not want to be labeled as being too fat or not looking gorgeous enough. Terms like "leftover lady" or "pork chop" lady are common derogatory nicknames for women who do not fit the stereotype in China.

Photo 4: This Chinese woman wears a traditional Chinese style outfit called *qipao* (旗袍).

This obsession with beauty explains why artificial surgeries are popular across China. Even for women not willing to undergo surgery, feminine, beauty remains a lucrative global market. Many Chinese women wear Chinese traditional style outfit called *qipao* (旗袍) to enhance their femininity (see Photo 4).

Beauty Products in China

Leading Western companies for example, are major players in China's beauty industry. The sale of beauty products accounts for a majority of Procter & Gamble (P&G) business in China. P&G's fastest-growing brand is Olay, famous for soap and body lotion. The amount of its business in China is comparable to that of business in the US with other beauty products. The company reports its sales in the 21st century have

Photo 5: Wedding photography is a huge industry, allowing couples to dress up in elaborate outfits and create idealized images of themselves.

grown by double digits. MaxFactor and CoverGirl cosmetics are among its product lines contributing to this success (see Photo 5).

These global names are not confined only to large cities like Beijing, Shanghai, and Guangzhou. More and more "smaller" cities with millions of consumers that were virtually unknown to the West just a decade ago, are now offering new opportunities for international companies to grow in China. China has more than 100 cities with over one million people. Thanks to urbanization, such cities represent an open well from which foreign companies can draw potential customers. To maximize that opportunity, Estée Lauder and other leading beauty companies either already own or are planning to invest in research and development centers in China.

For example, in early June 2012 Estée Lauder opened a new Research & Development center in Shanghai. Its main focus was to create products specifically for China. That was a departure from long-standing product procedures where the initial research was done in New York and then applied worldwide. Another distinction was that Estée Lauder's products developed in China could be exported for the global market. Therefore, Chinese women can set global beauty trends instead of just following them.

Success and Looks

Another reason manufacturers are eyeing the Chinese market is because they are aware that women in China see a direct link between success and looks. Euromonitor (2012) reported that increased spending power in China has been accompanied by growing demand for more sophisticated products. Therefore, consumers traded up in beauty and personal care products. The top five companies to benefit from these societal factors are P&G, L'Oréal, Shiseido, Unilever, and Amway. Other potential "players" probably will be encouraged to find the new market for aging adults in China (Euromonitor, 2012).[1]

Heal Yourself

Another part of looking good is staying healthy. Health-related industries have become a significant part of China's landscape.

The emerging middle class is working in an array of technical, management and professional occupations that demand not only skills but also long, working hours, and commitment to their job. This has led to greater stress and tension for these professionals. As a result, many may burn out both mentally and physically. At the physical level, stress causes muscle pain, backaches, and mental lethargy. All these symptoms impact greatly on the work performance, social life, and well-being of the individual. Large corporations know this and have explored different services and products to cater to them.

---

[1] Euromonitor (2012). The Greater Spending Power in China has been Accompanied by Growing Demand for Sophisticated Products. Retrieved on 18 June 2012 from http://www.euromonitor.com/.

Increasingly, holistic medicines have caught the imagination of big and small corporations as well as the elite.

Historical Context of Health Tourism

The use of natural wonders for health purposes is not new. For example, the physicians of ancient China had a long and rich history of using nature to cure the human body and promote better well-being. In recent decades, the trend is to engage in health tourism. Europe has a longer history of developing health tourism. The ancient Romans constructed thermal health spas and the English had health resorts as early as the 16th century. The poor sanitary conditions across Europe from the 15th to 17th centuries promoted an interest among the wealthy to develop medical spa's, mineral springs, and beach resorts for health and rejuvenation. This trend continued into the 18th and 19th centuries (Holden, 2006).

It was not until the late 1950s that the term "*wellness*" was introduced into people's speech. This word, developed by American physician Halbert Dunn, combines individual wellbeing and fitness. The concept of wellbeing requires determination and a change in lifestyle (Nahrstedt, 2004). While Asian systems of medicine such as Ayurveda, traditional Chinese medicine (TCM), yoga and tai chi recognized the wellness aspect of health centuries earlier, it planted the seeds of the concept "health and wellness" (Alter, 2005; Islam, 2009). Wellness is defined as "physical activity combined with relaxation of the mind and intellectual stimulus; basically a kind of fitness of body, mind and spirit, including the holistic aspects". Wellness is an element of human health recognized by the World Health Organization's (WHO) definition: "health is a state of complete physical, mental, and social well-being and not merely the absence of disease or infirmity"[2] (WHO 2000: 1978). Thus,

---

[2]WHO (2000). Health Issues in Developing Countries. Retrieved on 31 May 2012 from http://www.who.int/en/.

the merging of wellness and tourism is increasingly important for people worldwide.

The Nexus of Old and New

"Wellness and spa tourism" is one of the fastest-growing sectors of the Chinese tourism industry. Many people both domestic and abroad come to China for rejuvenation, alternative treatment or therapies offered by massage centers, village circle clubs, wellness centers, and other health tourist resorts. Wellness and spa treatment resorts have become a common tourist destination in China. The massive growth of resorts, spa, and vacation housing under private ownership is also a significant trend. Many resorts are located on beach fronts and carry out aggressive marketing campaigns to attract international health tourists. Most visitors coming for health tourism take part in wellness and spa activities for medical or rejuvenation purposes. Their clientele are mostly upper middle and upper classed Chinese, as well as people from Hong Kong, Macao, Taiwan, tourists from Western countries, or wealthy and affluent Chinese living overseas. The wellness packages are targeted at professional middle and upper class clients with disposable income.

Spreading the word about such activities is also essential. Service providers repeatedly broadcast advertisements over various media. They portray a new image of wellness and a healthy life that their clients can enjoy. They offer a broad variety of options. Packages include physical exercise, tutorials about healthy life, yoga sessions, various massage therapies, and dietary regimens, among other activities.

There are several reasons for the increased global advertising and spread of health tourism during the 20th century. First, the world has an increasingly aging population. Second, health and spa movements in early 1990s gave a push for more health-oriented facilities. The third contributor is the differences in healthcare systems worldwide, especially in cost of treatment, legality of select health procedures, and insurance coverage. The number of older individuals (60 years or above) is estimated to triple globally by the year 2050. This would be an increase from 606 million today to nearly two billion. This is a stark difference from over half a century ago. For instance, in 1950, persons aged 60 or over constituted 8.2% of the world population while in 2000 it grew 10%, and it projected to exceed 21% by the year 2050 (*ibid.*). As people grow older, they become more conscious of their physical wellbeing. This encourages many to travel to meet their health needs. Long waiting lists for treatments in many developed countries and medicinal expenses push ordinary citizens to go abroad for medical care. Prices vary between continents and world regions. A cataract operation in Britain costs around US$4,500 (£2,250), and in France US$2,250 (£1,125), but in India only US$345 (£173). With such differences in price, it is no wonder many are going to developing parts of the world for medical treatments. In addition, Chinese medicines are said to help consumers feel younger (Photo 6).

Photo 6:   Chinese medicines shops are common and offer a wide variety of herbs, fungi, and natural treatments and cure-alls.

Types of Medical Tourism

Medical tourism services are generally divided into three categories: invasive, diagnostic, and lifestyle. Bookman and Bookman (2007) explains that invasive medical tourism refers to procedures that are generally performed by specialists for people with non-communicable diseases such as dental care, plastic surgery, delicate eye surgery, cancer treatment, and joint replacement (pp. 43–44). These operations usually require advanced technology and machinery. Diagnostic medical tourism includes blood screening, bone density testing, heart stress tests, lipid analysis, and electrocardiograms. It is becoming a booming industry in recent years particularly in developing countries. Most of the clients are travelers from the West (*ibid.*). Lifestyle medical tourism covers a broad spectrum of services such as wellness nutrition, stress reduction, weight loss, anti-aging, pampering, etc. Lifestyle medicine combines traditional forms of healing or medical systems with the high tech exercise machines. This comes in the forms of yoga, Ayurveda in India and Thailand, acupuncture in Thailand, Malaysia, and the Philippines (*ibid.*).

Just as medical services provided vary, so do the tourists. Some of these differences include the client's country of origin, patterns of medical services they seek, motivation for healthcare, gender, and affordability. Further, there are two types of healthcare based upon the length of stay: long-term tourists, and ordinary tourists. Long-term tourists include students, migrant workers, or expatriates working in multinational or national enterprises in a country different than their homeland. Also, it includes retirees from relatively developed countries who moved to less developed countries. Ordinary tourists who seek healthcare in a foreign country includes those who travel for a short period of time to enjoy more tourist attractions such as beaches, jungles, monuments, historical sites, theme parks, etc. They have a high possibility of becoming ill while traveling since they are exposed to more high-risk activities.

Bookman & Bookman (2007) notes that apart from business deal making, many business travelers seek health care in foreign settings (pp. 45–48). Medical tourists seeking medical tourism are another significant category of health tourists which vary in terms of gender, income, age, race, and country of origin. Rich and poor patients consume different types of health care. For example, wealthy international patients demand high-tech services accompanied by an exotic vacation. Sometimes, this combines holistic medicine with modern technology. On the other hand, poor international patients tend to cross the border to use another country's health care services because of the unavailability or poor quality of services in their own country (Bookman and Bookman, 2007: 48).

New-Age Health Movements

With so many options available to consumers, it is no surprise that beauty and health are also up for some changes. Some scholars believe that over the last few decades a "new age movement" emerged that created an awareness and desire for a healthy life. Accordingly to Heelas (1996: 138), a group of people in the west established the "Counter Culture" movement as they "lost faith in the certainties of the capitalistic mainstream" (*ibid.*). New age appeals offered an alternative way to look at and perceive life. In the health profession, counter-culturalists "became critical of the capitalists medical establishment", especially allopathic dominance in healthcare (*ibid.* p. 141). Which focuses on symptoms rather than holistic treatments

Many patients are skeptical of Western allopathic medicine, which is more systematically planned and based on clinical diagnosis. Patients have reported feeling isolated from participation in decision making about their own treatment because of their lack of scientific knowledge and understanding of Western allopathic treatment procedures (Laws, 1996: 205). In contrast, alternative medical programs, such as those of health tourism, give patients comfort because of moral support from staff and other parents (Laws, 1996: 205). Health tourism also provides general health care and well-being for patients through restoring health (Connell, 2006).

Although health was traditionally considered a social service, today's consumer culture has reversed the "service content of health to commodity content". Today, especially in China, healthcare is viewed as a commodity and individuals are defined as its consumers. People's state of health is used in advertising and promoting health, spa culture and health tourism. Investors frequently portray images of slim, bronzed, and fit people enjoying an active social life (Laws, 1996: 202).

Moreover, this new age desire has risen from dissatisfaction toward modernity and capitalism. "Wellness and spa tourism", both new phenomena, are good examples of how human health is commodified for consumers in both China and overseas. This "culture" revolves around touristy health resorts that provide alternative medical and health services.

Conclusion

Beauty has always been an important element in most world cultures, but today it seems even more dominant. With the ease and popularity of cosmetic surgeries and other health products, it is a consumer-driven industry. Many of the women in today's post-reform China seek desine and ultimate wellbeing and beauty. They go to great lengths to maintain a lifestyle of beauty. Changes in working conditions in China for women have led to a burgconing industry of health spas and resorts. This new age tourism focuses on the overall physical wellbeing and satisfaction of its clients. China is leading the way in beauty trends which lends itself to new markets that have yet to be discovered.

References

ABC News (2008). Retrieved 13 January 2015 from http://abcnews. go.com/Politics/Vote2008.

Alther, J.S. (2005). Ayurvedic Acupuncture: Transnational Nationalism: Ambivalence About The Origin and Authenticity of Medical Knowledge. In Joseph A.S. (ed.), *Asian Medicine And Globalization*. Pennsylvania: University of Pennsylvania Press.

Bookman, M.Z., & Bookman, K.R. (2007). *Medical Tourism in Development Countries*. New York: Palgrave Macmillan.

Connell, J. (2006). Medical Tourism: Sea, Sun, and Surgery, Tourism Management, 27(6): 1093–1100. Contemporary Battle of the Classics'. *Journal of Classical Sociology*, 3(1): 67–96.

Euromonitor (2012). The Greater Spending Power in China has been Accompanied by Growing Demand for Sophisticated Products. Retrieved on 18 June 2012 from http://www.euromonitor.com.

Heelas, P. (1996). *The New Age Movement: The Celebration of the Self and the Sacralisation of Modernity*. Oxford: Cambridge, USA. Blackwell.

Holden, A. (2006). *Tourism Studies and the Social Sciences*. London: Routledge.

Islam, Md. N. (2009). New Age Orientalism: Ayurvedic Wellness and Spa Culture (under review). Paper Presented in British Sociological Association, London School of Economics. 6–8 April, 2009.

Laws, E. (1996). *Health Tourism: A Business Opportunity Approach*. In Stephen, C & Stephen, P.J. (eds.), *Health and the International Tourist*. London: Routledge.

Nahrstedt, W. (2004). Wellness: A New Perspective for Leisure Centers, Health Tourism, and Spas in Europe on the Global Health Market. In Weiermair, K. & Mathies, C. (eds.), *The Tourism and Leisure Industry*. New York: The Haworth Hospitality Press.

Chapter 9

The Legacy of "Leftover Ladies"

In many parts of the world, including the US and China, it is becoming more and more common to see unmarried women into their 30s. Many Americans do not see it as such a concern, but in China, singleness, especially for women, is still something frowned upon. The *Global Times* reported in 2001 that in Beijing alone, there were over 500,000 of these so-called "leftover ladies" or *shengnü* (剩女). Regardless of the growing number and negative sentiment, many of the Guangdong province women interviewed considered their lives more rewarding and liberating because they were single. These women were born in the 1970s and feel that, in post-reform China, they can make their own choices. But it turns it out they still face a double burden, caught between traditional values and modern thoughts.

What is puzzling is many of the women in this leftover status have more than enough men to choose from. In today's China, there are far more men than women, but these women simply choose to remain single. The Chinese Academy of Social Sciences (CASS) (2011) estimates that by the year 2020, a surplus of 30 million more men than women will be of marriage age in China. Most of the leftover ladies have high levels of education, good paying jobs, and enjoy their independence. Still, the Chinese media continue to promote the message that it is undesirable to have such a status.

The situation of Chinese leftover women is so extreme that in 2011, the All China Women's Federation under the direction of the Chinese Communist Party formally categorized sub-groups of "leftover women". The sub-groups ranged from age 25 as the "fight" and "hunt" for a partner group, age 28 as "they must triumph", ages 31 to 35 are "advanced leftovers" and age 35 and older were labeled as the "ultimate leftovers". Yan (2001) pinpointed that unmarried women have additional pressure which is the changing values of traditional gender roles and the Western views of womanhood. In turn, this causes society and parents to view leftover women in less favorable ways.

Single women in China experience difficulties because of their unmarried status, but much less explored are the views that these women have toward marriage. To (2013) studied the characteristics of leftover ladies from mainland China, Hong Kong, and Taiwan. Using the interactionist theory, she categorized single Chinese women's opinions of marriage into four groups: traditionalist, maximizer, satisfier, and innovator. Traditionalists view marriage as their highest priority, in a traditional sense, and look for a partner with a higher economic status. Maximizers are women looking for an "open-minded" Western-styled partner. Unfortunately, they usually experience a lack of family support for their marriage partners. Satisfiers believe marriage is important, but they have lower expectations in their marriage. For them, having a partner of lower social standing is not an issue. Innovators include those who just impulsively marry. Many women in this category pursue non-traditional relationships and prefer autonomy. To date, there are more and more ladies who choose to become single: *Shengnü* (leftover ladies). The appearance of *shengnü* in recent years has drawn the attention and interest of scholars, the media, and society. The term *shengnü* describes the country's group of unmarried women aged over 30, who are single, born in the seventies and "stuck" (see Photos 1, 2, and 3). Interesting names are given to those leftover ladies under different age ranges who are still single.

To (2013) asserts that leftover women's views of marriage result from the strict Chinese patriarchal structure. Most parents follow this traditional order and hope that their daughters marry within their same social class. This adds additional stress for women and it makes it even more difficult to find a marriage partner.

Research Methodology

The author used open-ended interview questions (both formal and informal) and an ethnographic qualitative approach to understand the women's feelings and views about marriage and their personal experiences (see Table 1).

The target population was 15 single women in mainland China, mainly in Guangdong province, Shanghai, and Beijing. All participants had at least a bachelor degree ($N = 15$), with 10 having master degrees ($N = 10$), one with a doctorate degree ($N = 1$), and one Juris Doctorate ($N = 1$). Most of the interviewees were living with parents. The researcher found participants using the snow-ball sampling method. All of the interviews were conducted from January to July 2014. The majority of interviews were conducted at their workplaces and others in cafés and restaurants.

The interview questions consisted of five parts. The first part elicited the interviewee's personal perception toward being single. In the second portion, the researcher asked their views toward getting married. The third section related to pressure from family members to get married and the fourth section was peer pressure from friends. Background information was also collected for further analysis. The researcher did a pilot test on two of the interviewees before the formal interview with the potential interviewees. From this pilot study, the researcher reworked the questions and revised them accordingly.

Guo is 34 years old and single. She works as a mid-level manager at a foreign bank in Beijing. She laughs about turning down dates and is already over the respectable age for marriage

Table 1: Demographic information for 15 in-depth interview participants

Name (pseudonym)	Age[1]	Qualification	Occupation	Monthly Salary (RMB[2])	Lives with Parents	Province
Apple	31	Masters degree	Flight attendant	8–10 K	✓	Guangdong
Betty	34	Masters degree	Dentist	10 K	✓	Beijing
Guo	34	Doctorate degree	Professor	30–40 K	X	Beijing
Gigi	32	Masters degree	Professional	10–12 K	✓	Beijing
Ivy	31	Masters degree	Bank officer	8–10 K	X	Shanghai
Jenny	39	Degree	Stock broker	20–40 K	X	Shanghai
Lily	40	Masters degree	Accountant	20–40 K	X	Shanghai
Ling	30	Masters degree	Professional	10–11 K	✓	Guangdong
Lucy	33	Masters degree	Technical officer	11–13 K	✓	Beijing
May	35	Degree	Pharmacist	20–40 K	✓	Guangdong
Mary	45	Juris Doctorate	Lawyer	10–20 K	X	Guangdong
Paula	31	Degree	Secondary school teacher	9–13 K	✓	Guangdong
Pinky	34	Masters degree	Lecturer	20–40 K	✓	Guangdong
Sung	33	Masters degree	Secretary	6–7 K	✓	Beijing
Yoyo	30	Masters degree	Editor	10–15 K	✓	Shanghai

(25–30 years). Once more, she does not want to make a hurried decision of marriage. She says "Marrying 'Mr Wrong' is even worse than being single. I have my own life, my own circle of friends, and my hobbies. I prefer to find my soulmate instead of finding a so-called husband".

Mary's story is one of heartbreak that led her to remain single even after age 30. She recounts that she was a junior lawyer in a law

---

[1] Age was based in the year of 2014.
[2] US$1 = RMB6.2. Retrieved from http://www.xe.com/?c=RUB#.

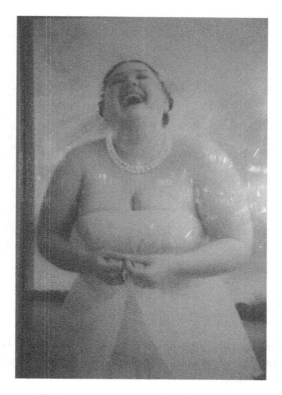

Photo 1: **For most Chinese women, marriage is an expectation. Even though it is a socially constructed norm, society looks down upon large women.**

firm in Jiangsu province in her 20s. She was fully dedicated to her career. "I barely stopped to see a movie, let alone get involved in a relationship", said Mary. After her two-year long relationship went sour, she moved to Australia. Where she obtained her Juris Doctor degree. She quickly got a job in a British industrial design company as their senior lawyer. Then the pressure to get married started. Mary's parents were so desperate they hired matchmakers. All of their hard work was pointless. "I wouldn't compromise by marrying a guy I didn't like", she said.

From the interviews, many of the so-called "leftover ladies" did not see themselves as such individuals. Instead, they saw it as a ploy

Photo 2: Many couples dream up fantastical weddings. But in the 21st century the majority of women over the age of 30 find some satisfaction in being a "leftover" lady.

used by the media to make them think less of themselves. Many still find enjoyment in their single lives and prefer to wait for a soul mate, companion, or confident instead of a husband. Many had high expectations for a prospective marriage partner and chose to be single. In terms of expectations, men with PhDs from abroad were perceived to be the perfect match for single Chinese women's expectations.

Indeed, most of the so-called leftover ladies had strong social networks of friends, who were in similar circumstances. They felt that there was no time to feel lonely. Many of these women spent time together at restaurants and other establishments. Furthermore, many leftover women recounted that in their mid-20s their parents worried about their marriage prospects, but now that they are over age 30, the pressure has lessened. Many parents respected their

Photo 3: **Chinese women value being thin, have black hair, large eyes, and have passive natures.**

decision to remain single, citing that it is mostly out of their control. Certainly, the young generation has strikingly different marriage patterns than those of their parents. Some of these changes in lifestyle include are reflected in statistics showing increased divorce rates, fears about childrearing, and access to higher education for women; all of which contribute to postponed marriages and thus leftover ladies.

Moreover, the expectations of marriage and wholesome family life was once paramount in traditional Chinese society, but today's times are different. Compared with women of previous generations where divorce was unheard of, the younger generation does not see the significance of marriage. The Ministry of Civil Affairs[3] (2007) cited that there were 2.1 million divorces in China. This is nearly

---

[3] Ministry of Civil Affairs, (2007). Divorce Rate in China. Retrieved on 12 May 2012 from http://english.gov.cn/2005-10/03/content_74343.htm.

seven times more than the rates in the 1980s. Because of these statistics, Jenny was cautious when choosing a mate. She recounted:

> Stressful work, an increasing divorce rate — there are many reasons leading career women [to] live on their own. The influence of material factors on marriage is diminishing among today's Chinese career women. Horrendous divorce stories lower my expectations about marriage (Jenny, 38, Stock Broker).

Her experience was echoed by many of the women her age. Most of them have had a bad experience before and they are afraid to be hurt. They stigma remains in their minds.

> There are no benefits for getting married. I'm not able to think of any one. For me, marriage is a strict and huge responsibility. Marriage is not for two people, it is for the two families. You have to communicate with others, and I don't want to do such extra thing. Marriage is only a sheet of certificate, it is not very useful. From my first love until now, I have never thought of getting married. It is due to my character that I don't think I need to do so. I am very independent (Mary, 45, Lawyer).
>
> Finding the right person is very important. After several attempts, it is impossible for me to find my man. I am afraid to be hurt again. Getting along with the other person is very difficult and it takes so much time to find. I am not adventurous enough to find my Mr. Right (Sung, 33, Secretary).
>
> I always play mah-jong with my friends. We sometimes go out to have a drink. I feel happy and enjoy my life now. I don't feel lonely." I go and eat out with my friends. They are also single. We have much fun together. Friends are enough for me. I don't feel alone (Jenny, 39, Stock Broker).

Another barrier for many women is the notion of childrearing. Many of the single women associated marriage with children and childrearing. They saw it was a large financial burden and family responsibility. The women estimated that it would cost them about

US$520,000 (RMB$3,224,000; £316,078) to care for a child from age 0 to age 21.

> The good thing about getting married is that I can have a partner to share things with and give birth to babies. But at the same time, I will lose my freedom and I have to cope with more stress. I don't really like babies and I don't think China is suitable for bringing up a baby. It takes time, money, love and patience. It is not an easy task to do so. I am the kind of person who likes to stay alone (Yoyo, 30, Editor, 30).
>
> If I don't really want to have a baby, I don't really want to engage with marriage. I would lose my patience to raise up a baby since there are not too many rooms for a baby to grow up in China (May, 35, Pharmacist).

The final contributor to Chinese women postponing marriage is higher education. Many leftover women reported having a masters or PhD degree, which gives them less time to date and look for a marriage partner. Many even study abroad, compounding the situation. For example, women might see local Chinese men as uneducated and the men might feel intimidated by the woman's high educational credentials. Such beliefs about education are culturally grounded. Mottos such as the following are held by both men and women as truth:

> If you have a bachelor degree, you are *Huang-rong*. Meaning: she is beautiful, intelligent and easy to communicate with.
> *Benkesheng shi huangrong* (本科生是黃蓉)
> If you have a master's degree, you are *Li Mo-chou*. Meaning: she is intelligent and good at *gongfu* but quite difficult to get along with other people.
> *Shuoshisheng shi limochou* (碩士生是李莫愁)
> If you are a PhD holder, you are *Miejue shi tai*. She is very good at *gongfu*, but she is very eccentric. She is superbly terrible to talk and communicate with.
> *Boshisheng shi miejue shitai* (博士生是滅絕師太)

Other participants expressed their views toward higher education for women and its impact on their relationships. Ivy was a professional from a middle class family in Guangdong province. She had a boyfriend and shared, her experience

> I personally think that guys from the outset focus on my physical appearance, figure, body and personality. It doesn't relate to my talents or abilities. It took me several years to look around and then I finally selected this guy as my boyfriend. But most of the Chinese guys are stressed now since they need to pay for the bills if they dine out with their girlfriends. They need to buy apartments if they want to get married. They also need to feed their parents and grandparents. Luckily I am not a PhD student. I won't pursue a PhD since this will become the burden on me in finding my husband. My parents told me that a Master's degree is sufficient enough for me right now (Ivy, 31, Bank Officer).

Another component of education was the location. For some of the women, it was difficult to find a mate because they studied abroad. Betty got her bachelor's degree in Guangdong province, China, but she earned her master's degree overseas. She said,

> If you can speak fluent English, this makes many Chinese guys run away. In Guangdong, not too many guys can speak and write good English. But if some guys can speak fluent English, they are our dream boyfriends or husbands. But I can say, in our company, actually, I cannot find any good-quality guys. I prefer a foreigner to a Chinese guy since most of the foreigners are more interesting, and have a sense of humour.

These are different times and present different challenges. Home ownership and financial stability seem to top the list of single women's expectations. Lucy got her MA in Hong Kong and presently works in Beijing. In her experience, women from her generation are richer than men. She valued being independent and working, even after being married. She expressed:

> I foresee I need to have my full-time job after I get married. I don't have any fantasies. I cannot fully rely on my husband. I cannot act like my mother who never worked after she got married. She is a housewife since she was only 20. But now, I expect if I get married and have children, I need to work. My future husband cannot afford all the expenditures if I don't work. I want to be financially independent as well (Lucy, 33, Technical Officer).

Although Lily was married, she supported Betty and Lucy's views. She held a full-time job while raising her children. Lily stated:

> I don't want to rely on my husband since I can work. I want to have my own salary to buy all the merchandise. I like branded goods and diamonds. Otherwise, I need to ask my husband to buy. I feel embarrassed if he refuses to buy some materialistic things for me … (Lily, 40, Accountant).

Many of China's single women are highly educated and economically stable. They have the means to get married, but for now, they enjoy their single status. This trend diverges greatly from that of their mothers and grandmothers. The *shengnü* are most common in urban cities such as Shanghai and Beijing. *Baike Reports* (百科報告), a Chinese web-based encyclopedia, cited in 2008 that there were already over half a million *shengnü* in China.

Conclusion

The situation of leftover ladies in China is multifaceted. The three most common reasons for postponing marriage were fear of divorce, hesitation in childrearing, and pursuit of higher education. The results from interviews indicated that the majority of leftover ladies fell into the category of maximizers meaning they seek marriage partners that are foreign-born and have an equal educational status as themselves. The parents of this generation have become more understanding of their situation and eased up the pressure. The single women of today's China are developing themselves and enjoy their unmarried status in ways that earlier generations could never have imagined.

However, the leftover ladies still suffer from the dilemma between traditional Chinese values to get married and being modern. They prefer freedom and individuality. On the other hand, they suffer from traditional Chinese values, i.e. they are mindful that Chinese society still expects women to get married before 30. And the life long career of a women is her family.

References

Chinese Academy of Social Sciences (CASS), (2011). *Dangdai Zhongguo Shehui Jieceng Yanjiu Baogao* (Research Report on Contemporary Chinese Social Strata). Beijing: Social Science Literature Press. [In Chinese].

Ministry of Civil Affairs, (2007). Divorce Rate in China. Retrieved on 12 May 2012 from http://english.gov.cn/2005-10/03/content_74343. htm.

To, S. (2013). Understanding *sheng nu* ("leftover women"): The Phenomenon of Late Marriage among Chinese Professional Women. *Symbolic Interaction*, *36*(1): 1–20.

Yan, Y. (2001). Practicing Kinship in Rural North China. In McKinnon, S & Franklin, S. (eds.), *Relative Values: Reconfiguring Kinship Studies*. Duke University Press, pp. 224–243.

Chapter 10

The Crisis of Masculinity
of the Ant Tribes in Post-Reform China

In sociology of gender, there are lots of studies focused on women. The female perspective was extensively explored in great detail including their stories of life in post-reform China. We discussed leftover ladies, and female education in post-reform China in the previous chapters. Masculinity has not been given the same scrutiny. Especially regarding masculinity, economic reforms, and socio-cultural norms. This chapter explores the ongoing debates in Sociology about masculinity. The author contends that the masculinity crisis of the "ant tribes" (university graduates who work in blue collar jobs) must be placed within a socio-cultural framework that accommodates local Chinese culture.

This chapter begins by describing the "ant tribe" crisis. The chapter then provides the theoretical framework for understanding the issue. These sections highlight the Sociology of masculinity, socio-cultural perspectives of masculinity, and first-hand accounts with ant tribe members. The last part investigates ways in which the masculinity crisis results in lack of home ownership and delayed marriage. It concludes that different kinds of social policies and institutions like *hukou, danwei* are closely intertwined with a number of cultural and social practices in deciding the ant tribes' chances for life success in reform-era China.

The "Ant Tribe" Crisis

On the surface, many Chinese men experience similar circumstances as their Western counterparts and have similar aspirations such as getting married and raising a family. In this context, the ant tribe crisis is also a "masculinity crisis" for a group of low-paid college or university graduates in Chinese cities who have migrated from rural areas. Si (2009) refers to these low-salaried blue-collar workers with high qualifications and university degrees as "ant tribes" or *yizu* (蚁族). This inability to find employment causes difficulties for these men to get married, raise a family, and own a home.

Research Design

From 2010 to 2013, the author conducted in-depth and semi-structured interviews and participant observation with 20 rural-born men from the ant tribes from five cities across Guangdong province, Guangzhou, Shenzhou, Zhongshan, Zhuhai, and Yangjiang. They originally come from different parts in China. The author chose rural-born men because they had more difficulty finding employment in China. Many lacked the urban *hukou*. The men ranged from 23 to 38 years old. All 20 participants were single and half reported having stable girlfriends. Some interviewees worked in a factory, while 12 were blue-collar workers such as technicians and factory workers. These men have grown up in a highly materialistic culture, with little political influences, and hope for a bright future, and secure jobs.

Unfortunately, they differ from the new Chinese middle class' younger generation in several ways. Firstly, they lack English language proficiency, which makes them less marketable (Tsang, 2014). Secondly, they work, but the majority of them reported earnings of around RMB3,000–6,000 (US$385–US$770) per month. Most of them are workers or clerical officers in factories or multinational companies. This makes it nearly impossible to rent, let alone buy a house in Guangdong.

The in-depth interviews were conducted in both Mandarin and Cantonese Chinese and based on open-ended questions, focusing on (1) their reasons to come to Guangdong? (2) their feelings about working in non-traditional occupations for men and with little means to upgrade their intergenerational mobility (3) their coping strategies in Guangdong (4) their plans for getting married, purchasing a house, and raising a family (5) their opinions toward traditional Confucianism values including: male superiority, forming a family, and producing heirs. Each of these questions were analyzed through various sociological theories to better understand the life experiences of the ant tribe men in post-reform China (see Table 1).

Theoretical Framework

Bradley (1999) and Lin (2013) suggest that gender relations are not only problematic, but can also be negotiated and contested. They have differing levels including individual, organizational, cultural, and societal levels. Post-structuralism has impacted gender relations because it presents gender categories as more contradictory, fragmented, and open to multiple meanings (Barrett & Phillips, 1992; Butler, 2004; Fraser, 1997; Kelan, 2010). The author argues that a post-structuralism lens is not enough to fully understand the gender relationships impact on the masculinity crisis in post-reform China. Rather, a socio-cultural approach to gender studies better explains the crisis of masculinity in today's China. It can be explained by the specific socio-culturally embedded factors like social institutions (structure) and cultural distinction (agency).

Table 1:   Profiles for the ant tribes

Name (pseudonym)	Age[1]	Qualification	Occupation	Monthly Salary (RMB[2])	Native Place
Jiang	23	Bachelors degree	Worker	3K	Yunnan
Wei	25	Bachelors degree	Worker	4K	Jiangxi
Li	24	Bachelors degree	Worker	5K	Lijing
Wang	25	Bachelors degree	Worker	4K	Chongqing
Wu	32	Bachelors degree	Teller	3K	Hunan
Zhang	34	Bachelors degree	Worker	3K	Henan
Xu	36	Bachelors degree	Worker	4K	Chongqing
Ye	32	Bachelors degree	Worker	4.5K	Anhui
Jie	35	Bachelors degree	Clerical officer	5K	Guizhou
Sun	34	Bachelors degree	Worker	4K	Guizhou
Yu	38	Bachelors degree	Clerical officer	5K	Shenyang
Ming	29	Bachelors degree	Worker	4K	Shangdong
Lin	25	Bachelors degree	Worker	5K	Henan
Ma	28	Bachelors degree	Worker	5K	Nanjing
Yang	28	Bachelors degree	Worker	4K	Hunan
Wei	23	Bachelors degree	Technical officer	5K	Sichuan
Leng	38	Bachelors degree	Technical officer	6K	Shangdong
Wing	37	Bachelors degree	Worker	5K	Zhejiang
Feng	36	Bachelors degree	Technician	5K	Guizhou
Fan	28	Bachelors degree	Technician	5K	Sichuan

[1] Age was based in the year of 2014.
[2] US$1 = RMB6.2. Retrieved from http://www.xe.com/?c=RUB#. Retrieved 30 November 2014.

The multiplicity of the masculinity crisis of the ant tribes is the result of diverse and contradictory forces of oppression within specific institutional areas and Confucian values like *wen* (being intellectual), *wu* (being physically masculine), and being a good son. The significance of state power (structure) comes into play in affecting professional skills. Social connections shape class formation and reproduction (agency). The tribe members are contextualized among the state, the market, family relationships, and traditional values; it becomes clearer as to their techniques for navigating such a complex environment. Struggle, redefinition, and accommodation give way to a range of possibilities for these men and their Confucian practices to drive their lives (Kong, 2011: 195).

In post-reform China, the seemingly antiquated Maoist social institutions of *danwei* (work unit 单位), *hukou* (household registration 戶口), and non-family-based interpersonal networks (*guanxi* 关系) continue to affect the lives of ant tribe members. Ant tribes do not have urban *hukou* status, which equates to no influential *danwei* (work unit or political affiliations). Thus, for these men it is impossible to develop *guanxi* networks with influential cadres, ex-cadres, and cadre-business people (Tsang, 2014).

People who are privileged enough to have *hukou* and *danwei* status, reap material benefits from powerful social networks. But for the ant tribes, not even parents can help their sons get social mobility (Tsang, 2014). The vicious downward spiral is that, because of their less than satisfying situations, ant tribes postpone marriage. This deteriorates their masculine images and identities of manhood even further. This is an extreme loss of face (*lian*) and is a highly unwanted situation for any person in China.

Sociology of Masculinity

One might wonder what defines manhood and men. Masculinity generally refers to a set of qualities identified with men: they possess superior physical strength and financial independence, work in manly jobs, and are the breadwinners of their family (Connell, 2006). Floge & Merrill (1989) note that much of a man's future is determined by his occupation and career path. Masculinity also means achievement and status, self-reliance, strength, aggression, and homophobia (Levant & Kopecky, 1995). Because many ant tribes lack monetary wealth, they remain unmarried and see themselves as less than masculine. For many males, their self-images are diminished because they see their circumstances incompatible with traditional Confucian norms about fatherhood and carrying on one's family name.

The post-structuralist approach to gender studies emphasizes that gender has categories and is contradictory, fragmented, shifting, and indecisive (Butler, 2004; Kelan, 2010). Through exposing the constructedness of supposedly natural behavior, gender takes on new meanings, which lead to a range of defined identities. Changing norms related to gender and sexuality broadens the topic even more. In some respects, gender might well be the apparatus by which such terms are deconstructed and denaturalized (Butler, 2004). Butler proposes new ways of understanding gender. This makes it possible to critique the topic (Butler, 2004; Kelan, 2010).

The multiple forms of masculinities and femininities do not imply physical changes, but instead focuses on the cultural identity of men and women. For example, a man might act feminine, but physically he is still a man. Through such an example, new concepts of gender and gender relations by post-structuralist theory have only made the original concept more convoluted.

When studying gender relations and identity, it is important to consider the interplay of power, gender, class, sexuality, and ethnicity. This intersectionality has found it is difficult to distinguish whether ones identity is more important in a situation. Moreover, Andersen & Collins (2003) suggest that such practices can lead to reverse forms of oppression (p. 185). However, the ways the gender categories and divisions are more contradictory and form multiple meanings is still problematic because different contexts result in different results. This perspective puts into question the validity of the "traditional genders" and presents multiple options for individuals (Kelan, 2010: 190).

Socio-Cultural Perspective on Masculinity

The post-structuralist approach to gender relations identifies new ways of undoing gender. However, in the context of post-reform China such a study must also incorporate the local institutional and cultural practices that are at play. Socio-cultural factors such as social institutions, traditional cultural values, and norms directly influence class, status and mobility in Chinese society, and therefore, cannot be ignored. A gender relation is the intersection where power, stratification, desire, and identity formation meet (Lin & Mac, 2013: 499). Within different contexts, gender relations act in other ways. Socio-cultural perspective on gender studies brings together social institutions (structure) and cultural practices (agency). As mentioned earlier in this chapter, the social institutions refer to the Maoist tradition of *hukou, danwei*, and *guanxi* and continue to be active in the lives of the ant tribes. The cultural practices are what individuals based upon the institutional parameters. Work situations in China have changed as a result of *hukou* and *danwei*. Furthermore, *guanxi* networks create social stratifications. Relationships or *guanxi* networks can only be established within the one's class boundary. With this in mind, *danwei* contributes greatly to upward mobility in urban China. Parents of the ant tribes have some options by nature of their age and historical context, but they lack the education and monetary means of advancing socially in today's China (Tsang, 2013). This makes it unfeasible for the benefits to be passed onto the ant tribes' generation.

The Maoist ideology is not the only one moving Chinese society. Louie (2002) believes that traditional Confucian forms of masculinity *wen* and *wu* also motivate many Chinese and their norms. *Wen* signifies refinement and academic achievement, while *wu* represents physical strength and military strength. Both *wen* and *wu* masculinities are acceptable and sought after. Although, post-reform China is drifting slowly away from these Confucian attitudes and a more materialistic individualism, many ant tribes they feel they are failing at upholding these cultural and social expectations of what it means to be a man (Lau & Kuan, 1988; Leung, 1996).

Masculinity Crisis of Ant Tribes

With the changes in social values in across post-reform China, one might assume that individuals will change with society. However, that is not the case. Since economic reforms in 1978, many migrant workers from poorer parts of rural China have migrated to urban Guangdong province. In the 1990s there was a burst in university students competing for white-collar work. The oversupply made many recent graduates jobless. Globalization and economic reforms have only added to the unemployment problem. Thus, many of the available jobs, especially for men are non-traditionally masculine occupations such as bank tellers and non-managerial positions. Many of the ant tribes do not have high proficiency in English language, they lack competitive professional skills in the form of qualifications like Chartered Financial Analyst (CFA),[3] the Association of Chartered Certified Accountants (ACCA),[4] Certified Public

---

[3] CFA is a very prestigious and professional credential offered by the US-based CFA Institute. A candidate who successfully completes the program and meets other professional requirements is awarded a "CFA charter" and becomes a "CFA charter holder". CFA Institute is the global association for investment professionals. For more details, see the website of the CFA Institute at http://www.cfainstitute.org/programs/cfaprogram/Pages/index.aspx. Retrieved on 4 March 2014. The CFA examinations are demanding and the pass rates are not especially high. In the period 2002–2012, the 10-year weighted average pass rates for Level 1, Level 2, and Level 3 examinations were 39.7%, 44%, and 51% respectively.

[4] ACCA is the highest qualification for accountants. Holders of this internationally recognized qualification can work for professional accountancy companies.

Accountant (CPA),[5] or other professional degrees. Without these credentials, it is almost hopeless to earn a high salary and status in society. Worse yet, the ant tribes' parents lack the social *guanxi* to help them make sufficient connections and networks for higher employment.

For example, Jiang, a 23-year-old migrant worker, graduated with a degree in Finance and Marketing from a university in Yunnan. His hometown is a small village near Lijiang (an eight-hour train ride from the capital city of Kunming). He came to Guangdong to pursue his dream of becoming a white collar professional or a manager. He arrived in Shenzhen in 2010, but even after 12 months of job searching he found nothing. His frustration led him to work in a low-end factory. Jiang said,

> I think since I just got a bachelor degree I did not expect to be a 'king' right away. But I felt at least I could find a decent job, like sales or clerk. I never tell my parents I have to become a factory boy. It is so shameful. It would break up their hopes and expectations of me. I could never imagine I would have to compete with women to work in the garment industry. Can you imagine we had to sew more than 80 pairs of jeans per hour? It sounds amazing that I could accept these gruelling, miserable conditions that made me feel like a slave. I am the breadwinner in my family for my parents, grandparents and brother. My brother needs me to send him money to go to the university. My parents are farmers who find it hard to earn enough just to live in their hometown. I don't have the choices or skills to secure a better paying job (Jiang, 23, Worker).

Jiang struggled with the high expectations from their parents. He felt bad that his parents invested so much money into helping

---

[5] CPA is a statutory title of a qualified accountant who passed the examination of the Uniform CPA. Only those CPA holders are qualified to provide attestation, usually including auditing opinions on financial planning or statements.

him get higher education, but not end results of a strong career. Wei, 25, Jiangxi, has a story similar to Jiang's. He said,

> I need money to feed myself as well as to make a living. After you were employed for one year, you do all the dirty jobs. Dignity, face, and masculinity are cheap. I have no extra money to learn more English and improve my professional qualifications. Making a living is the top priority. I always say, a dirty job is always better than no job (Wei, 25, Worker).

From the interviews of Jiang and Wei, many members from ant tribes have to cope with both financial and emotional difficulties as they try to support their families. For them, earning money is more important than saving face and following the prescribed masculine jobs. These men did auxiliary-service work, which were low paying retired women's jobs. Jiang shared that he felt abandoned and marginalized when he worked in such jobs. Other men felt pressure and frustration from being the only son and unable to support their family. Some even wanted to commit suicide.

To evade these feelings, Jiang hid the fact that he was working as a factory boy. In every way possible, he had to show his masculinity. However, at present Jiang, Wei and the rest of the factory boys had to develop strategies for coming to grips with this new (male) understanding of traditionally classified "female" jobs (Simpson, 2004). These factory boys had to apply relational gender ideology as they transitioned their masculine identities into perceived female vocations.

This transition meant that they needed to be accommodating in their relationships with managers and bosses. They had to be flexible, obedient, and adaptive to their new environment.

Li, 24, a factory worker from Lijiang (in Yunnan), said,

> The Smartphone assembly line is routine, boring, and it hurts my self-image and dignity as a man. This job is very tedious and meticulous to details. I feel sorry for my parents who supported

my tuition fees. I have a bachelor's degree, but I have to work in factory. What an idiot I am! (Li, 24, Worker).

Lin, aged 25 and worked in a Smartphone factory who comes from Guizhou. He concurred with Li. He felt dehumanized and upset he lost his manhood and masculinity. He said,

> I feel useless and ashamed. I am competing with women. I am in charge of the warehouse. All the heavy jobs passed to me. But I share the same pay with women and women usually are allocated light jobs like sitting in front of the assembly lines. Sometimes, I feel very depressed, emotional, and want to commit suicide (Lin, 25, Worker).

In traditional Chinese culture, masculinity has a greater "social utility" than femininity. This causes many men to maintain control and power, which is socially achieved through culture, institution, and persuasion. The ant tribes believe in cultural capital, masculinity and manhood, but being a factory boy is problematic because it quite the opposite, femininity. The Chinese version of factory worker is not the same as that in the West, where heavy lifting or other manual labor tasks are performed. Instead, the in China, factory work is very tedious and involves making delicate clothing or other products, which are more feminine oriented. As Simpson (2004) says, this causes many men to feel anxiety because they are not performing in their proper gender role (p. 365). For many of the ant tribe men they feel their manhood is undermined by working in such female-oriented jobs.

Navigating the Masculinity Crisis in Post-Reform China

The author believes that the challenges faced by many ant tribes stem from socio-cultural problems (*hukou, danwei,* and *guanxi*) in China. Most of the ant tribe members interviewed had at least a bachelor degree. However, cultural capital alone was not adequate to guarantee their career success because they lacked trust-enhancing *guanxi* networks. These elements are essential for access to white-collar jobs.

In this study, the ant tribes lacked close ties with cadres, professionals, and entrepreneurs and without urban *hukou* status they had no insurance protection. The situation was compound because the registrations are organized by place of birth. The men in this research were exclusively from the countryside and migrant status. This is nearly impossible to change.

Wang, aged 25, graduated from Chongqing Normal University with a degree in Electronic Engineering and came to Guangzhou for better opportunities. In 2009, he worked as a publicist for a media advertising company. His maximum income from commissions was RMB7,000 per month (about US$1,000 per month). Generally, the basic salary was only RMB2,000 per month (US$322 or £196). His average monthly expenses were above RMB3,000 (US$483 or £294) and even after five years of working, he still did not have a bank savings nor chance for promotion to be a manager. He felt his finance degree was useless because he was an outsider (*waidiren*) to the people of Guangdong. The locals would not trust him to handle cash and company secrets.

A similar situation was Wu, aged, 32, graduated from a university in Hunan province who had been working as a bank teller in Zhuhai since 2008. He once had dreams of buying an apartment Zhuhai and bringing his parents to live with him. But he earned less than RMB5,000 a month. After 6 years he felt burnt out with no hopes of upward mobility. He said,

> I want to become a manager but I find the chance is slim. My bank doesn't trust me as an outsider (*waidiren*) and I don't have money to upgrade my skills like learning English or other professional qualifications. Most of the promotions are given to local people since they have better bargaining power for upward mobility. I get stuck here and it seems I have nowhere to go (Wu, 32, Clerical Officer).

Zhang, 34, comes from Henan, concurs with Wu. Local urbanites described these two ant tribe members, Wang and Wu who come from the countryside and usually have a backward looking. Most of people think the outsides one being lazy, stupid, incompetent, of a lower class, and agrarian. Even the way they dressed, spoke, and carried themselves signaled that they were from rural status or *suzhi*. They tried to blend into the consumer culture of the city, but they remained as outcasts and ostracized from society.

This present catastrophe has its roots in the early Maoist social institutions such as *hukou, danwei*, and *guanxi*. Chan (2009) adds that these are an active determiner of one's intergenerational mobility in post-reform China. *Hukou* registrations varied between rural and urban, locals and non-locals, benefits and no benefits (Lee & Yang, 2007).

Danwei (work unit) refers to the place of employment, especially to urban state enterprises and administrative departments during the pre-reform period (Lü & Perry, 1997; Bray, 2005). Moreover, this system is credited for facilitating *guanxi* networks inside class boundaries (Wu, 2002). Without the protection of urban *hukou* and *danwei*, most of the ant tribes could not have *guanxi* connections. Thus, the ant tribes get paid low salaries because of their non-resident status. Without access to local social security, most of the ant tribes cannot receive their pensions and receive healthcare coverage. The ant tribes must be very innovative in their approach to coping with these institutionalized challenges.

Masculinity Crisis: Buying a House and Postponing Marriage

Another aspect of the masculinity crisis of the ant tribes is home ownership and postponing marriage. In the Chinese context, having a home is a prerequisite for finding a suitable marriage partner. For many of the men interviewed, they expressed embarrassment and shame for not being able to uphold cultural expectations. Many of these men were not in a position to support their families, let alone own a home, and get married. The first part of this section will describe the plight of home buying followed by the marriage difficulties faced by the ant tribes.

The property market in China had severe problems and caused the plight of many of the ant tribes. Government sponsored renewal projects compounded the issue. In 2010, the cost of rent was only RMB800 (US$129 or £79) per room. But by 2013 that rate nearly doubled to RMB1,200 (US$193 or £113). Not surprising, none of the men interviewed had a house in urban Guangdong.

Over three years Jiang, Zhang, Li, Wang, and other ant tribe members moved across Guangdong province under a government sponsored urban development program. Because ant tribes did not have urban *hukou* status, they could not apply for low-priced government housing. Housing and real estate booms caused this problem. Working-class buyers have been frozen out of the market, while an estimated 65 million apartments across the country (bought as speculative investment) sit empty (Tan, 2013).

Wang worried aloud whether he would be able to marry his high school sweetheart, who accompanied him to urban Guangdong. Yet, five years later they still do not own a house. Such concern is rampant among ant tribes. The traditional Chinese cultural value demands that a groom provide an apartment for his bride. Wang said "I'm giving myself two years". His voice trails off. Although they wanted to get married, right now achieving their dreams appeared futile.

Compounding their situation, many ant tribe members must deal with the stress of finding a marriage partner. The participants in this study shared their parents' worry because they were still single and in their 30s. Many ant tribe parents are so desperate to find wives for their sons that they resort to matchmaking. This is a cheap alternative to the expensive payment for professionals. They stand outside of the city squares and display their son's photo trying to find some eligible leftover woman. In addition, most parents have saved money so that their sons can afford to buy houses and get married.

Xu, aged 36 and a factory worker, recalled his first visit to his girlfriend parents' home in Chongqing. Her parents asked Xu about his salary and his nesting plan. Xu informed his future mother-in-law that at the present time, he was unable to buy a home. The parents did not seem impressed by this. Soon thereafter, she dumped him.

Clearly, men and women alike have been socialized into their unique gender roles. Ye, aged 32 from Anhui, told the researcher that women in mainland China have been socialized to believe that they are the primary providers of money and security. Thus, as part of this natural order men should provide women with materialistic comforts, such as a house. Jie is from Guizhou, he is a 35-year-old clerk and he said:

> Girls commonly ask questions like to do you have a house or are you living with your parents? What is your job? How much did you earn? Do you have a car? Are you a professional? It is very difficult to find girls who want to eat in KFC or McDonald's. Who will consider me? I have three 'lows', 'low' salary, 'low' status, and 'low' height (Jie, 35, Guizhou).

Sun is aged 34 and the only son in his family, and he comes from Guizhou. He agrees with Jie. He said,

> I have lots of expectations from my parents, relatives, and society. Buying a house and forming a family are the top priorities for a man. I still think that failing to get married is a sign of a bad son and disrespectful to my parents and relatives. Who is going to inherit my bloodline (*xiemai* 血脉) in my family? I lose my *lian* (face 臉) in front of my relatives and family members (Sun, 34, Guizhou).

The interviewees agreed that the masculinity crisis was interwoven with the Confucian expectation of what it means to be a masculine "man". From this philosophy, a person is defined as a relational self within a structured, socially reciprocal relationship network.

The pressures to own a house, get married, and continue the family bloodline are signs of a good son and a good man. The ant tribes are required to deal with their family positions or *lian* (臉), and *mianzi* (face 面子) of their families. For many of these "ant tribe" men, their identity is formed by the family and friend structures (Kong, 2011).

While *mianzhi* (面子) is the social face, *lian* (臉) is the social prestige that comes from one's actions (Hu, 1994). Thus, for a man to lose both *lian* (臉) and *mianzhi* (面子) is viewed as shameful for not only himself, but also his family and Chinese society. Halberstam (2005) notes that the ant tribes are transient people who live in a "queer time", "outside of reproductive and familiar time as well as on the edges of logics of labor and production" (p. 10). For many ant tribe members, they still want to fulfill these masculine roles. Many of these men dream of raising a family and have sons to inherit land in their rural hometowns, but for now that dream sees very distant. Their inability to make strong connections compounds their circumstances, but they are adjusting to the changing times across China.

Conclusion

This chapter examined the masculinity crisis of ant tribes in post-reform China. It provided both a sociological framework and a socio-cultural perspective by bringing in the importance of *hukou*, *danwei*, and *guanxi* for the ant tribes in Guangdong. The author contended that the current masculinity crisis amongst the ant tribes could only be understood by using a socio-cultural perspective. This chapter also questioned the efficiency of Chinese higher education and the study of latent social problems such as crimes or violence against women.

Men from ant tribes felt compelled to uphold the traditional values of masculinity and the inherent superiority of being a man in post-reform China. However, the harsh reality for many of these men was that they lack skills, status, and family connections or *guanxi* for getting ahead. Despite having college degrees, the ant tribes were forced to accept jobs perceived to be feminine or blue collars. Many were not competitive enough to become successful in Guangdong. This bleak situation limited upward social mobility and eroded their self-esteem. This has contributed to the massive Chinese masculinity crisis and the maintenance of traditional values, social institutions, and social ties shape the lower class behavior and mobility.

References

Andersen, M.L., & Collins, H.P. (2003). *Race, Class, and Gender: An Anthology*. Belmont, CA: Wadsworth.

Barrett, M., & Phillips, A. (eds.), (1992). *Destablilizing Theory: Contemporary Feminist Debates*. Cambridge: Polity Press.

Bray, D. (2005). *Social Space and Governance in Urban China: The Danwei System from Origins to Reform*. Stanford: Stanford University Press.

Bradley, H. (1999). *Gender and Power in the Workplace*. London: Macmillan.

Butler, J. (2004). *Undoing Gender*. London: Routldege.

Chan, K.W. (2009). The Chinese *hukou* system at 50. *Eurasian Geography and Economics*, *50*(2): 197–221.

Connell, J. (2006). Medical Tourism: Sea, Sun, and Surgery, Tourism Management *27*(6): 1093–1100. Contemporary Battle of the Classics'. *Journal of Classical Sociology*, *3*(1): 67–96.

Floge, L., & Merrill, D. (1989). Tokenism Reconsidered: Male Nurses and Female Physicians in a Hospital Setting, *Social Forces*, *64*(4): 925–947.

Fraser, N. (1997). *Justice Interruptus: Critical Reflections on the Postsocialist Condition*. New York: Routledge.

Halberstam, J. (2005). *In a Queer Time and Place: Transgender Bodies, Subcultural Lives* (Sexual Cultures). NYC: New York University Press.

Hu, H. (1994). The Chinese Concepts of — Face. *American Anthropologist, 46*: 45–64.

Kelan, E.K. (2010). Gender Logic and (Un)doing Gender at Work. *Gender, Work, and Organization, 17*(2): 174–194.

Kong, S.K. (2011). *Reinventing the Self under Socialism-Migrant Male Sex Workers* (Money Boys in China), London. Routledge.

Lau, S.K., & Kuan, H.C. (1988). The Ethos of the Hong Kong Chinese. Hong Kong: Chinese University Press.

Lee, C.K, & Yang, G. (2007). *Re-envisioning the Chinese Revolution: The Politics and Poetics of Collective Memories in Reform China.* Washington DC: Woodrow.

Leung, K. (*1996*). The role of beliefs in *Chinese culture*. In Bond, M.H. (ed.), *The Handbook of Chinese Psychology*. Hong Kong: Oxford University Press, pp. 247–262.

Levant, R.F., & Kopecky, G. (1995). *Masculinity Reconstructed: Changing the Rules of Manhood — At Work, in Relationships, and in Family Life*. New York: Dutton.

Lin, X. (2013). Filial Son, The Family, and Identity Formation among Male Migrant Workers in Urban China. *Gender, Place and Culture*.

Lin, X., & Mac, A.G. (2013). Chinese Male Peasant Workers and Shifting Masculine Identities in Urban Workspaces. *Gender, Work and Organization, 20*(5): 498–511.

Louie, K. (2002). *Theorising Chinese Masculinity*. Cambridge: Cambridge University Press.

Lü, X.B., & Perry, E.J. (1997). *Danwei: The Changing Chinese Workplace in Historical and Comparative Perspective*. Armonk, NY: M.E. Sharpe.

Si (2009). Yizu. Daxue biyesheng jujucun shilu 蚁族. 大学毕业生聚居村实 Guangxi: Guangxi Normal University Press.

Simpson, R. (2004). Masculinity at Work: The Experience of Men in Female Dominated Occupations. *Work Employment Society, 18*(2): 349–368.

Tan (2013). Retrieved on 28 August 2014 from http://www.tealeafnation.com/2013/07/new-report-sparks-discussion-of-chinas-bachelor-crisis/#sthash.G91JLcEw.dpuf. Retrieved 21 October 2014.

Tsang, E.Y.H. (2013). The Quest for Higher Education by the Chinese Middle Class: Retrenching Social Mobility? *Higher Education*, *66*(6): 653–668.

Tsang, E.Y.H. (2014). *The New Middle Class in China, Consumption, Politics and the Market Economy*. London: Palgrave Macmillan.

Wu, F.L. (2002). China's Changing Urban Governance in the Transition Towards a More Market-Oriented Economy. *Urban Studies*, *39*(7): 1071–1093.

Chapter 11

Corruption and Green NGOs in Post-Reform China

As with any changes in a country, there is destined to be room for inappropriate and dishonest behavior. This chapter begins by providing some background related to the corruption issues that face China's post-reform political sphere. Following this information, this chapter will present various case studies from interviews illustrating corruption within both government and non-governmental organizations (NGOs) and the involvement of the new middle class. Later, this section will explore Green NGOs (GONGOs) and their involvements in bribery activities. It will also discuss the relationship that the green and business NGOs develop some kind of *guanxi* networks with the Chinese new middle class.

Within the realm of China's government, corruption is widespread. One landmark situation involved the railway system. In 2011, the former deputy chief of engineering for China's Railway Ministry was arrested on charges that he had stolen US$2.8 billion and deposited these funds into foreign bank accounts. Just a few months after that official's arrest, China's Central Bank posted a report charging that 16,000 to 18,000 public officials had fled China since the mid-1990s, taking with them an estimated US$120 billion. This report was deleted soon thereafter by government censors.

However, problems which related to corruption continued to surface in 2012 when Chinese authorities arrested the President of the Postal Savings Bank of China (PSBC), on suspicion of economic dishonesty. This was not the first of such scandals that have affected China's banking system. A few weeks earlier, an executive Vice-President of the Agricultural Bank of China (ABC) was also arrested. The Communist Party and the central government say it is all part of a larger campaign to eradicate widespread corruption. In an earlier speech, even Chinese President Hu Jintao admitted that corruption is a problem. He said: "If corruption does not get solved effectively, the party will lose the people's trust and support".

Ironically, back in 2010 the head of China's anti-corruption force was sentenced to death (with a suspended sentence) for engaging in corruption himself. Even the military is under scrutiny. Officers must disclose all sources of income as well as real estate properties. Also, it is mandatory to report all investments in the "Standard Declaration of Personal Matters" to the government. Officials claim the officers' information will be checked under improved verification procedures. In the past, military officers have been notorious for using their status to benefit for their own financial situation.

The leading form of corruption in the government is embezzlement of funds for personal gain. In an article in the *Wall Street Journal*, Pei (2012), a Professor at Claremont McKenna College, suggests that the Chinese government has grown softer on corruption since 2000. "In the Chinese case", Pei says "corruption has made food unsafe, increased income inequality, worsened environmental degradation, reduced social services, and resulted in widespread abuse of individual rights. If we take the low quality of life in China into account, the pernicious impact of corruption is substantial". Certainly, these destructive acts have not ceased, regardless of government involvement.

China Economic Weekly states that over the last 12 years, an estimated 18,487 officials, including executives from government-owned companies, have been caught trying to flee overseas with illegal money. Another report by the Washington-based watchdog Global Financial Integrity, which tracked illicit outflow of money by all people, not just officials, found China led the world with US$2.7 trillion (five times as much as runner-up Mexico) illegally taken out of the country from 2000 to 2009 (*China Economic Weekly*, 2012).[1]

It seems no level of government is exempt from corruptive practices. During China's economic boom of the 1990s, even local officials had made changes that promoted corruption. In return, this led to more bribes or *tanwu shouhui* (貪污受惠) and the use of public funds for personal gain or *nuoyang gongkuani* (挪用公款). For many local government officials, they have a fixed salary regardless of their performance. This makes them more likely to engage in corruptive behavior. Many use government funds for personal gain, but in turn use those monies to buy products, which stimulate China's economy. This makes it increasingly difficult for the central government to monitor local politicians and their activities.

Because local government is essential to economic prosperity, "special businesses" rely on specific connections in order to operate. "Special businesses" include hotels, tour agencies, fitness centers or salons, karaoke bars, massage parlors, sauna baths, and other entertainment establishments. These are quota-restricted business, so licenses are difficult to obtain from the License Registration Bureau. In Guangdong province, it is easy to run a "normal" business, but running a "special business" (*tezhong hangye* 特種行業) is especially difficult. Local authorities employ quotas on the number of entertainment clubs, hotels, travel agencies, bars, discotheques, restaurants and coffee shops, and massage salons in geographic areas. Strong social connections with regional party cadres are essential for

---

[1] *China Economic Weekly*, (2012). Corruption in China. Retrieved on 14 April 2012 from http://www.ceweekly.cn/common/english.html.

starting up a "special business". Thus, owning a licensed "special business" implies that the business owner has strong *guanxi* with local authorities. A connection with a strategically placed cadre is the most effective and efficient way to enjoy additional benefits.

From interviews with entrepreneurs in Guangdong province, they confirmed that such activities are usual in business licensing matters. Here is Uncle Cheng's story[2]:

> Although getting business licenses isn't difficult, it can be very troublesome and complicated. The procedures are pretty complicated and bureaucratic. I tried for ten years before successfully getting one with the help from one of my very good friends. He introduced me to a cadre. Everything can be settled through referrals and meals. The trade-off is to give red packet and gifts to the cadres. The cadre helped me by arranging all matters about the setting up of the factories in a smooth, efficient way. If you want to get licenses for special industries in Guangdong, it is extremely difficult (Uncle Cheng, 40, entrepreneur).

From these accounts, it is clear that corruption is a serious problem in post-reform. In its Corruption Perceptions Index, Transparency International[3] gives China low marks and claims that the root of China's corruption stems from "the misuse of public power for private benefit". This is not the only factor according to Global Integrity. It reports that China's restrictions on information (including the media) are the cause of widespread corruption. Under this index, China gets a rating of weak in its anti-corruption efforts.

In 2010, Global Integrity felt hopeful of China's prospects, when the Communist Party issued a new code of ethics to fight against widespread corruption. The organization has also been

---

[2] The interview with Uncle Cheng in this chapter was conducted by the first author in 2008.

[3] Corruption Perceptions Index, (2011). *Corruption*. Retrieved on 12 April 2012 from http://cpi.transparency.org/cpi2011/results/.

pleased with the rise of anti-corruption websites in China. Such sites encourage people to share stories of bribes in an online forum. On many occasions, these "citizen journalists" have promoted the government to take action. Regardless of these well-meant efforts, corruption still thrives across China.

China's NGOs

Government is not the only sector suffering from issues of corruption. A great deal of bribery occurs within non-governmental organizations or NGOs. China's NGOs, organized by government or not, have spread nationwide under the country's socio-economic reforms. They have become so popular that the government has allowed them to prosper, even to the extent that they too have been cited for corruption. Nonetheless, this has stopped the development of other forms of NGOs. With increasing environmental concerns, it becomes no surprise that the government would create NGOs to solve its problems.

Environmental NGOs (GONGOs)

Strong economic growth in China has led to increased concerns for the environment. Many of the Chinese new middle class studied by the researcher admitted that they had misallocated resources not for environmental NGOs, but instead, they were busy strengthening their business networks with cadres and multinational corporations (MNCs). Like any organization, it is built upon strong connections. In recent years environmental NGOs or GONGOs have been thriving across the country thanks to local and provincial government strong relationships with the new middle class. These relationships are seen as practical and reciprocal. The middle class is unwilling to confront the state that is still in control of scarce resources necessary for doing business. To avoid social conflicts, members of the middle class remain quiet and support policies from the Chinese government.

Despite the deteriorating environment in Guangdong, many GONGOs do not make any attempt to decrease the problem. In theory, such groups are to work together and solve environmental issues, but in South China this has yet to happen. Most GONGOs are not keen on doing environmental work. They do not regulate or monitor other GONGOs either. Instead, most staff members seek their own interests and extending their *guanxi* networks. They usually line up with professionals and overseas entrepreneurs to set up MNCs in the province, and have part-time jobs in or act as consultants to the multinational corporations. GONGO officers reveal that while the Ministry of Environmental Protection and regional Environmental Protection Bureaus (EPBs) are dedicated to environmental protection, there is a disconnect with the local governments on carrying out their work. Currently there are no penalties for officials who do not comply.

With such activity being common, the Chinese government created an independent body called the Anti-Corruption Bureau in 1989.[4] This agency investigates local enterprises and environmental officials in their practices and holds them accountable to GONGOs. Yet, the effectiveness of the Bureau is debatable. It does not have any influential role to play in protecting the environment, particularly in newly developed industrial areas. There is no supervision of it.

From interviews with local officials, many claimed that corruption is more rampant from within the Bureau than outside of it. Because much of the public (government responsibilities) and private spheres (enterprise operations) are so interconnected, it allows many practices to be overlooked.[5] Percy, the director of one GONGO,

---

[4] See Zhonguo fan tan ju — zai tansuo zhong qianxing, (2004). China's Anti-Corruption Bureau: Forging Ahead While in Search of the Route to Success. Retrieved on 18 November 2011 from http://news.sina.com.cn/c/2004-03-02/14032985447. Retrieved on 15 July 2014.

[5] Beach, M. (2007). Local Environmental Management in China. *China Environment Series*, 4: 21–31.

recalled that his colleagues allowed a foreign entrepreneur to invest less than US$1 million to set up factories near the Pearl River Delta region, which intentionally dumped industrial waste into local waterways.[6] This is only one of many similar scenarios that are taking place across much of Guangdong province.

Because many government officials at various levels are deny industrial pollution and dumping of foreign e-waste in China, it is easy for GONGOs to also disregard any environmental problems. GONGOs cannot avoid the temptation from MNCs to extend networks in doing business.[7] Peter, a full time staff member in a GONGO, was wary of his seniors who often used the resources in his work unit for their personal benefit. His words explained why GONGOs do not deter associational growth in South China:

> My boss does not allow me to use the name of our GONGO for my personal benefits. But most of our colleagues [six out of eight] contact the donors or clients to extend their own networks. I do whatever I can to build up networks (with green NGO and MNCs), but of course not for the puny salaries. In fact, most of my time, I am not helping our GONGO, but helping my boss to handle his part-time jobs (other business projects or consultancy work) with some MNCs.[8]

Problems Associated with GONGOs

From Peter's story, it raises questions about the effectiveness of GONGOs founded by the Chinese new middle class at truly fulfilling

---

[6] Personal interview, Guangdong, June 2008.

[7] For NGOs' Reliance on International Funding, see Tang and Zhan, [2008], Civic Environmental NGOs, Civil Society, and Democratisation in China: Journal of Development Studies. 44(3), 425–448. 431–432. See also Jude Howell, Getting to the Roots: Governance Pathologies and Future Prospects. In Howell, J. (ed.), *Governance in China*. Lanham, MD: Rowman & Littlefield Publisher, (2004), pp. 226–240.

[8] Personal interview, Guangdong, August 2008.

their role as environmental advocates. The interviews collected indicated that many leaders of GONGOs are from China's new middle class who wants to extend their *guanxi* networks, while using the name of GONGOs. Some middle class people and professionals set up GONGOs not because of environmental protection, but instead to attract the public's attention to environmental issues. GONGOs are believed to be the rallying cry for fundraising purposes and to readily win the sympathy of local citizens. Most importantly, NGOs create opportunities for middle class people to meet both MNCs and local officials. The interviews revealed that developing reliable personal connections with power-holders (cadres) was the main business strategy for young entrepreneurs and professionals. Collaboration within the same class also helped maintain individual and group interests.

Guanxi Networks and Bribery

As mentioned in previous chapters, *guanxi* network building and rebuilding have become internalized or *habitus* for the Chinese.[9] This puts a unique twist to interpersonal matters, where *guanxi* networks are central. Individuals use *guanxi* networks and various kinds of social capital to create a "cultural nexus of power".[10] This phenomenon was commonplace in the author's research samples in Guangdong. This research also found that the most powerful *guanxi*

---

[9] Elaborated by Bourdieu, P. (1984). "Habitus" refers to a set of socially learned dispositions, including ways of speaking, thinking and acting that are acquired by members of social groups or class by virtue of living in the same objective conditions. See his *Distinction: A Social Critique of the Judgment of Taste*. London: Routledge & Kegan Pau, and Giddens, A. (2009). *Sociology*. Cambridge: Polity Press, pp. 1120–1121.

[10] Cultural nexus of power means in order to build and use *guanxi* networks, most of the green (GO)NGOs and MNCs rely on their close relationship with each other to extend their business networks. Duara, P. (1988). *Culture, Power, and the State: Rural North China*, 1900–1942. Stanford, CA: Stanford University Press.

networks are those with police, local party cadres, and government officials. These individuals exert direct control over land use, financial resources, and law enforcement. For example, if entrepreneurs operate without business licenses ("special business" licenses in particular), they will be seen as criminals and subjected to all sorts of harassment by police and other authorities.[11]

In order to maintain a healthy relationship, private entrepreneurs usually offer consultancy services to or business collaborations with cadres, including those posted in GONGOs, in return. This model illustrates reciprocity and its impact in many people's lives. This kind of *guanxi* between GOs, NGOs, and MNCs are long-term. Therefore GONGOs prosper but they do not actually solve, or raise public awareness of environmental problems.

At the same time, GONGOs rely on connections with MNCs for their funding. With insufficient operating budgets, this makes ties even more important said according to Michael, the founder of a GONGO interviewed in this study. Donations usually come from enterprises rather than the government. Thus, good relations with enterprises help to raise funds for NGOs. Michael said:

> Right now, I have my full time job in one MNC. I got the job when I had collaboration with MNCs. But I am still keeping my GONGO simply because it is good to meet more MNCs and extend my network. I use part of my salary to run this green NGO. I run environmental campaigns and fundraising in order to draw more attention from the public. It is good for me simply because I can keep close relationship with MNCs. Also, it benefits MNCs as well because it is good to their business image.[12]

NGO organizers like Michael and Percy wish to set up their NGOs and build up their reputation with MNCs. Percy, who works

---

[11] Li, Z. (2001). Migration and Privation of Space and Power in Late Socialist China. *American Ethnologist*, 28(1): 179–205.

[12] Personal interview, Guangdong, August 2008.

for a GONGO recognized the immense competition in China, which makes *guanxi* networks so crucial.

> Now almost every Chinese is a degree holder, and the degree certificate is like an admission ticket to opening up a better career path. Given that everyone is the same as you are as a degree holder, you have to resort to *guanxi* to make yourself stand out. Luckily, I got a full-time job in a multinational enterprise through my *guanxi* network. At the same time, the MNC sponsors my GONGO to bolster its image and to be well recognized by local people … I would take some of my salary out to support and pay for the running costs of our group.[13]

Ken, a full-time staff member at a GONGO, echoed:

> I mainly help my boss to do his own personal job like seeking networks with different multinational enterprises in our NGO. We have frequent contact with GONGOs to do promotion and activities about AIDs or other civil affairs. But this is only the gestures [*zitai*] and promotions [*xuanchuan jiqiao*] … Our leaders do not want to set up a board of directors to monitor our daily practices. They don't want to have records … My boss does this for his own fame and for seeking *guanxi* network. In fact, little effort has been dedicated to promoting environmental awareness and production. They want to use GONGOs as a cover. In fact, my boss uses it a means to seeking cooperation with multinational corporations …[14]

Many GONGOs and MNCs do not frequently concern themselves with environmental or business ethics. Rather, the main working efforts of most NGOs and GONGOs in Guangdong province are focused on *guanxi* building to create strong social bonding among professionals, regional cadres, and entrepreneurs.

---

[13] Personal interview, Guangdong, July 2008.
[14] Personal interview, Guangdong, June 2008.

Conclusion

This chapter addressed the issue of widespread corruption both within the government and also in the non-governmental organizations or NGOs. Using data from interviews, it was clear that the use of GONGOs has served a different purpose than just simply to protect the planet. Instead, GONGOs have been set up more for the purposes of social bonding.[15] In post-reform China, most people are on a quest for social capital. *Guanxi* networks have become an institutionalized habitus. NGOs are often used as institutionalized sites for personal and organizational gains. This reveals the complexity of the exploitation within both the government and NGOs in post-reform China.

References

Pei, M. (2 May 2012). Minxin Pei: Communist China's Perilous Phase. *Wall street journal*. Retrieved on 28 August 2014 from http://www.wsj.com/articles/SB10001424052702304746604577380073854822072.

Tang, SY. & and Zhan, XY. (2008). Civic Environmental NGOs, Civil Society, and Democratisation in China. *Journal of Development Studies*. 44(3), 425–448.

---

[15]Coleman, J.S. (1998). Social Capital in the Creation of Human Capital. *American Journal of Sociology*. 94: 95–120; Lin, N. (1982). Social Resources and Instrumental Action. In Marseden, P.V. & Lin, N. (eds.), *Social Structure and Network Analysis*. Beverly Hills, CA: SAGE Publications.; Lin, N. (1995). Local Market Socialism: Local Corporatism in Action in Rural China. *Theory and Society, 24*(3): 301–354; Lin, N. (1999). Building a Network Theory of Social Capital, *Connections*, 22(1): 28–51; Lin, N. (2001). *Social Capital: A Theory of Structure and Action*. Cambridge: Cambridge University Press.

Chapter 12

Popular Culture, Media, and Society in Post-Reform China

This final chapter investigates popular culture, media, and society in light of post-reform China. The intersection of these elements reflects the importance of economic consumerism and the decline in political involvement. This has caused inequalities in urban and rural areas especially in China's rich second generation *fuerdai*.[1] Some rich people are called *tuhao* (rich but do not have manners 土豪). Many can afford to study abroad and they tend to stay in the US or the UK to work or study. They are largest consumers of pop culture and were born after 1980 and are the only child.

Popular culture encompasses many elements including fashion, consumerism, leisure, luxury, and much more. Brand goods not only have practical value, but they also serve as symbols of social status. This '80s generation grew up in the era of economic reform. Consequently, most of them have never known the hardship their parents experienced. They only know prosperity, which explains their lifestyles and expectations.

---

[1] *Fuerdai* (富二代) means the rich second generation young adults who are born to large family are eager to flaunt their riches. Many of these individuals can afford to study abroad and tend to stay in the US or the UK to work or study.

In China, pop culture echoes all things Western. The young people are driving this market. They are interested in not just films, music, and technology, but also the idea of what it means to be a consumer. The new generation are very Western, but with a twist of luxury. This is evident as one travels around China. Fashionable coffee shops like Starbucks, Pacific Coffee, and other western cafés dot the landscape. Even fast food chains like McDonald's, KFC, and Pizza Hut are easy to find. There are also many brand labels like Gucci, Prada, and Louis Vuitton. The young people's choice of electronic items would include Apple's iPhone. Even music choices would definitely include artists and songs that foreigners would recognize. It is all part of the Chinese pop culture (see Photo 1).

Most of the young generation feels up-to-date, trendy, and more energetic when interacting with its same age group. Thus, a common spot for the privileged few of the new middle class is bars, pubs, and nightclubs. By frequenting such places, these individuals feel they can "show off" their style and sell themselves to prospective business deals. In addition, a survey done by a public relations firm shows that young people will buy luxury items — even though they cannot afford them — simply to pamper themselves. Thus, in post-reform China the young generation has more opportunities for attaining cultural capital, social networks, and economic capital (Ministry of Industry and Information Technology, 2013).

Challenges within Post-Reform China

As with any opportunity come its challenges. Faced with skyrocketing housing prices, and scarce job prospects, social unrest becomes more pronounced. The widening gap between rich and poor, disagreements over social and personal values, and difficulties of finding a mate have added complexity to many people's lives. These conditions make it difficult for many to uphold cultural expectations for raising a family and caring for their aging parents.

The young generation cannot rely on the strategies of their parents' generation because much of today's China is institutionalized.

Photo 1: Blending Eastern tastes with Western Values?

Cultural capital such as education has become the gatekeeper for many positions, but it is worthless without the social capital and *guanxi* networks. Furthermore, the young generation's ideas about employment are different. Because they can choose their own career path, many feel liberated and seem to worry less about job security. For many, lifestyle and status are more important than actual work.

Media and Society

Another area affecting this generation of Chinese is new media and digital technology. This includes the Internet, mobile phones, and television. China has the largest Internet usage in the world. Statistics show that Chinese consumers spent 1.9 billion hours a day online. By 2015 the country is expected to add an additional 200 million users bringing the total to 700 million online. That is double the combined users in Japan and the US.

Although, popular American websites like YouTube, Facebook, and Twitter are blocked in China, Chinese language equivalents of these sites are popular and grown. More and more, young people share status updates and contact friends. One possible reason for social media's popularity stems from distrust of government-controlled media.

The mobile revolution is also transforming lives in China. Statistics show that two-thirds of China has mobile phones. The country's Ministry of Industry and Information Technology reported in February 2012 that there were more than a billion mobile subscribers in the country. Many homes in China have never even had landline phones. Some new research shows that almost 40% of China's Internet users get online exclusively from mobile devices like mobile and smart phones. Young people access the web on their mobile phones because these are quicker and more convenient alternatives to computers.

Another segment of technology is television. It has become less popular in recent years, with the advent of video and TV shows streaming online. Nonetheless, second to DVDs in stores, online is the place. Interestingly, many of the shows that are popular in the U.S. such as the *Big Bang theory*, *Gossip Girl*, *Sex and the City*, and *Prison Break* are also highly rated in Asia. There is a large network of volunteers who translate these shows into Chinese and some of the dialogue is changed to reflect cultural sensibility.

Although China's youth are keenly interested in all things Western, when it comes to ideological and cultural realms, they adhere exactly to the Chinese Communist Party. The rise of fan clubs in China is a typical example. The young generation knows that fan clubs can never be used as a tool to challenge the Chinese

Communist Party. Instead they use these clubs as a space to, in a general way, worship their idols like Jay Zhou, Lady Gaga, and others. The Chinese government allows the fan club culture to exist, as long as it does not provoke the Chinese government.

The Young Generation's Pursuit of their Individual Desires

China's growing interest in accumulating wealth is a hallmark of the young generation. Individualistic attitudes of conspicuous consumption are a response to the changing politico-economic climate in China. Individualism has displaced political ideals and social morality. These imported values from pop culture create a context for the formation of a culture of pleasure.

A new array of social perils, such as over-spending and materialism are undermining traditional Chinese norms. But for the young generation in today's China, those values are something of a different era. The young generation of China's middle class will continue to play a major role in developing China. The extent to which they are successful will probably depend on their use of social, economic, and political capital to forge a new path to China's success.

Reference

Ministry of Industry and Information Technology (2013). Announcement of Industry Merging Guidelines: Beijing, China, Ministry of Industry and Information Technology Joint Announcement.

Conclusion — Rethinking Global Governance: Chinese Model in the Making in the 21st Century?

This book provides background regarding China's early Mao Era in the 1950s leading up to the reforms in the late 1970s. It related to the changing and transforming Chinese society. It then explored post-reform China from various socio-cultural perspectives. In particular, macro structures such as the One-Child Policy, family and marriage, women, and the emergence of the Chinese new middle class were at the forefront of these categories. Within these were subtopics of in situational structures (*guanxi, danwei*, and *hukou*), corruption, left-over ladies, beauty, health consumption, and youth culture. Thus, Chinese society has undergone a series of dramatic transformations in almost all realms of social, cultural, economic, and political life. This book has attempted to elaborate, in simple terms, the multidimensional issues that today's China is facing.

Today, China and its people look forward to the future, there are several areas which require further exploration and study. These challenges for China include banking, currency, intellectual properties, the One-Child Policy, and the new Chinese middle class. By addressing these critical issues, China will be in position to lead the world in many areas of both culture and economics.

Banking

China's banking industry is experiencing many challenges. Private companies in China have trouble borrowing from state banks since most of their lending generally goes to the state-owned enterprises or SOEs and on favorable terms. This has led to many cases of fraud and embezzlement. The solution would seem to be to allow more foreign banks in the country, but party leaders have been reluctant to ease regulations. Foreign banks could provide the much needed access and capital to Chinese businesses and individuals. This could possibly sustain China's continuing growth.

In addition, China's state-controlled banking system has trouble. In 2009, banks were ordered to make massive loans to local government projects in order to avoid a recession. Analysts feel much of this money went to waste. As a result, banks had to write off bad loans. Local governments could not afford to bail them out because their main source of revenue from land sales dried up.

In the past, banks got away with weak lending practices because they earned large profits from deposits. Thus, with the expansion of deposits, it has allowed Chinese banks to outgrow bad debt. Savers, who received negative real interest rates on their deposits, subsidized banks. They had little choice because capital controls prevented them from taking money offshore and they had nowhere else to put their money. But changes in the system and *guanxi* connections have changed that.

As China's connections with the outside world have grown, the government's control has also weakened. The new Chinese middle class who own major shares of deposits, has been moving capital abroad. Declines in the country's foreign exchange reserves and RMB deposits in Hong Kong imply that the amount of capital going elsewhere is on the rise. Banks can no longer get away with supplying cheap capital for wasteful investment projects. China's main export markets are weakening and its current account surplus is vanishing. What worked for the government in the past will not work anymore.

To accommodate these changes, China needs to upgrade its international banking procedures. While Hong Kong is in step with the rest of the world, the mainland is not. Foreigners consistently find that simple international wire transfers are a painful task. What might take 10 or 15 minutes in the US can take a half hour or *more* in China. The system seems obsessed with unnecessary paperwork. Since the number of foreigners in the country continues to grow, this must change. If it does not, China will lose its competitive advantage on the world stage.

Currency

A closely related area to banking is currency. China's business partners criticize the government's tight regulation of the RMB. They want to see it be allowed to float and respond naturally to market conditions. It might be to China's disadvantage on the export market. By holding down the value of its currency, it has made Chinese exports to the US cheaper and American exports to China more expensive. Chinese leaders have consistently identified the need for new currency policies based on the market, but it has yet to do so. This could force the government to pay more attention to its domestic market.

Intellectual Property

The manufacturing sector, is facing challenges regarding intellectual property. Many countries have accused China of violating international laws in its trade policies and not upholding intellectual property laws. China is known as the world's largest producer of counterfeit goods. Pirated films, DVDs, and music CDs top the list of problem areas. Many top American entertainment industries have complained about this many times. China will need to learn how to balance its practices and those of the world system to enjoy the maximum benefits in the future.

China's One-Child Policy and the Aging Population

China's One Child Policy is leading to social welfare issues. Most younger Chinese are struggling to make ends meet. They often do not have the financial opportunities like those from the 1990s, but are still expected to support their aging parents just like in the past. If the child cannot provide this help, the Chinese government should implement some sort of uniform social welfare. Also, the aging population leads to concerns about pension plans. Whichever path the government takes to tackle this issue it will most likely be costly.

Labor

The aging population, coupled with the One-Child Policy creates concerns for available workers in China. With respect to labor itself, China should continue reforms of the *hukou* (household registration) system. Workers need to be able to move more freely and respond to the needs of the job market. The current *hukou* laws should allow citizens to freely move around China without risking their rights to education, social services, and the housing market.

Other Population Needs

As China continues to grow, households will demand that a larger fraction of national income goes into consumer goods. Presently the government is acquiring investments and foreign reserves, such as U.S. Treasury Bonds. Spending on consumer goods accounts for only 35% of China's GDP compared to over 70% in the US. This might lead some Chinese to feel disconnected from the system and seek a stronger voice in political arenas.

Social Unrest

Social unrest across China is likely to continue. Each year there are probably thousands of protests in the country, many in rural areas. Most instances involve government land speculation of villagers' property for development purposes and usually the villagers do not receive adequate compensation. Other times, migrants complain about low wages and discrimination in housing, education, and healthcare. Urban unrest is also common in factories across Guangdong province. If China is to keep the peace in cities and to continue to attract migrants, it needs to provide them with equal rights as local urban dwellers.

Aside from the specific incidents, each one has a theme: discriminatory government rules and actions. Even China's security chief has warned that the country is "ill-equipped" to deal with social unrest. These issues must be solved democratically and in a timely manner in order to bring more social cohesion.

The New Middle Class

With stark differences between the middle and working classes, China needs to balance its support of these two classes. Over the past 15 years, the middle class has almost blindly supported the Chinese government and benefited greatly. Economic growth led China to global powerhouse status and consumer wealth. But today, many analysts believe that China's economy is slowing down.

The middle class hopes to continue its lavish lifestyle. Today's middle class has money and influence to demand action. The future may depend on both political and economic reforms. Possibly through close relationships with the central government, the new middle class can gain access to the once untouchable realm of politics. The extent to which the middle class supports or opposes the Chinese government will probably define the parameters for political reforms and its position as a world player. However, the orientation means that the middle class is fragmented and not able to pursue its common interests collectively. The constituents of the middle class thereby do not form and converge to a class that covers all entrepreneurs, professionals, and cadres. Instead, the middle class maintains particularistic coalitions that are competitive and take advantage of each other. Second, the middle class is fond of social comparison in order to rationalize its conspicuous consumption and ostentatious lifestyles. The basis of such practices rest on inequality and associated risks escalating in China (Qi & Oberwittler, 2009; Zhang & Mo, 2005). The inequality and risks in turn originate from marketization to make people competitive and aggressive (Boland, 2007). Consequently, the middle class demands safety, privileges, and differences from others to take advantage of inequality in society. The demand thereby underlies the quest for privileges and extravagance through the political-economic coalition. Third, the middle class is powerful economically and politically, particularly thanks to the hybrid forces of the market economy and authoritarian polity (Dittmer & Gore, 2001).

Property

In order to keep the middle class satisfied, property and land rights should be reevaluated. Under the current system, it is very confusing and raises questions about who actually owns property both in rural and urban areas. Moving forward, the party will need to sustain urbanization, which comprises a large part of the economy. China has been successful in attracting young underemployed rural residents to urban jobs. But with increasing demands, this labor supply may not be enough. China should attract other age groups, especially those from the countryside. As an incentive to move to urban areas, farmers should be able to sell or mortgage their land.

But the party is skeptical of privatizing farmland to farmers mostly for fears of a poor migrant population but also ideological reasons.

In more urban parts of China, the residential real-estate market is an area of concern. After years of overbuilding, millions of apartment complexes remain empty. In 2011, housing supply exceeded demand by nearly 50% (UBS). Most people believe that real estate will rebound as soon as policies are changed. But the trends in the US, Spain, and Ireland suggests that overbuilt housing markets take years to correct. A similar situation could happen in China as well.

Politics

Politically, China is facing some challenges between hard party-liners and reformers. There are expected to be some leadership changes in the country, but it is unclear whether the government will choose the usual tactics or change.

Environment

In light of China's rapid development, environmental issues have been a concern for many. The government needs to make *"growing green"* a priority and not just something on paper. Most cadres and the middle class prefer to cooperate with foreign enterprises for monetary purposes, but at the expense of heavy industrial waste polluting nature. Therefore, controlling China's high pollution rate is a major issue for years to come.

Corruption

A final threat to China's economic success is corruption across all levels of government. Within local and provincial government, there have been many instances in recent years of money swindling, bribery, and false accusations. The Chinese government has attempted to address these issues by creating anti-corruption and anti-conspicuous consumption laws. The central government is not doing enough to implement them and hold individuals accountable. This situation may only be the tip of the iceberg in China. Additionally, instituionalaized social elements such as *guanxi* have allowed cadres, entrepreneurs, and professionals to have close ties with party leaders.

On to the Future

Perhaps the best conclusion that can be gathered for China's future is that change is on the horizon. The forms and the stakes for such changes remain to be seen. It appears that the middle class will be the most affected by changes. Especially in the social institution of *hukou*, if people migrate and others get equal status, this will cause an increase in taxes and more people will become more active in politics. When compared with the students who led the Tiananmen Square protests in 1989, the new Chinese middle class has not been politically active. But they could be "sleeping giants". Their anxieties might grow into anti-government rage once they feel their privileges will be lost. If they begin to protest, the government will again have to decide if it will make changes or repress. If the government chooses the latter option, it may in turn make the middle class even more active politically. In other Asian countries, a greater appetite for freedom has come hand in hand with rising incomes. Thus, the best option for the government's path should be one of practicality and moderation.

The challenge of the Chinese government will revolve around its ability to make the middle class feel that they have a stake in its society, at least for now. The Chinese government will definitely encourage its citizens to focus on economic development and consumerism, but remain distant from political participation. This principle will most likely lead the Chinese government in the coming decade.

References

Boland, A. (2007). The Trickle-down Effect: Ideology and the Development of Premium Water Networks in China's Cities. *International Journal of Urban & Regional Research, 31*(1): 21–40.

Dittmer, L., & Gore, L. (2001). China Builds a Market Culture. *East Asia, 19*(3): 9–50.

Qi, C.H., & Oberwittler, D. (2009). On the Road to the Rule of Law: Crime, Crime Control, and Public Opinion in China. *European Journal of Crime Policy Research, 15*: 137–157.

Index